COLLECTIONS OF THE HEART

2020 Edition

The Book Binder Anthology

Copyright © 2020 The Book Binder/Merry Streeter

All rights reserved.

ISBN: 9798560770495

To our posterity,

May you know we,

your grandparents and parents,

thought of you with love and devotion.

Acknowledgments

I thank CrossWinds Church of Moreno Valley, California, for giving our writer's group a place to gather and grow as writers.

It became a warm huddle whereby we learned to sharpen our skills, smooth rough edges, and don the writer's cap with purpose.

These assembled writings represent a cornucopia of our life
as stories, poems, and devotions.

We bring you our tears & laughter, soul food and silliness, richness and gravity, believing this compilation will touch your heart.

To the prayer-writers who helped support this accomplishment during which time
many trials and setbacks were a challenge; thank you with all my heart and to God be the glory.

This compiler/author thanks all those who submitted their works
to make this anthology a bounty:

Jim Hutcheson, Cindy Tesar, Dennis Knotts, Sharon Miller, Phyllis Boles, Reina Dozier, Stella McDonald, and myself, Merry Streeter.

"The Book Binder Anthology 2020 Edition"

COLLECTIONS OF THE HEART

Together, we present--

"The Book Binder Anthology 2020 edition

COLLECTIONS OF THE HEART

Contents

Acknowledgments	i
Affairs of My Heart	8
BURDENS	11
CLOSE ENCOUNTERS OF THE BIRD KIND	14
CRYSTAL THE UNICORN	16
El Vale De La Muerte	47
FPB-M 927	55
Hard Rock Gold	61
HIRAM ON THE HEIGHTS	65
IN THE COMPANY	84
IT IS YOUR CHOICE	87
JAWING	89
Law West Of The Pecos	91
PHANTASMAGORIA	98
RESCUED BY AN ANGEL	108
SPRING TONIC	114
SUMMER OF 1945	123
The Accident	127
The Stairway (excerpt)	137
TODAY, THY NAME IS GRACE	143
A Child's Conversation with God	149

COLLECTIONS OF THE HEART

ALONE	150
An Ode to Ease the Bereft	153
A Christian Writer's Prayer	155
BRIEF THOUGHTS ON SIMON OF CYRENE	158
GIVE	160
Harried	162
Hearts That Touch	163
HURTFUL WORDS	165
The Encounter	167
My Heart's A Fraud	169
THE UNSEEN HEART	171
The Walls Of My Life	173
THUG	176
TO WHOM IT MAY CONCERN	178
SWEET SALLY BROWN	180
FIRE IN THE HOLE	183
"...Give Me This Mountain..."	186
God Dispenses the Wind	190
God Will Defend Me!	194
"I See You in Everything All Day"	196
Let's Start Stacking	199
Life Is A Vapor	201
Mistaken Impression	205
MY DREAM VACATION	207
The Arm Story	209
The Powerful Flow!	211

COLLECTIONS OF THE HEART

SPIN-THE-BOTTLE	215
SAGA OF TWO HORNS	218
Where Is Nowhere	220
Eschatology	228
AUTHORS	232
Phyllis Boles	233
Reina Dozier	234
Jim Hutcheson	235
Dennis Knotts	237
Stella McDowell	238
Sharon Miller	239
Merry S. Streeter	240
Cindy Tesar	241

COLLECTIONS OF THE HEART

SHORT STORIES

COLLECTIONS OF THE HEART

Affairs of My Heart
by Jim Hutcheson

In the fall of 1948, Kathy Bauer, a friend, brought Florma Foxen to Judson Baptist Church in San Bernardino to our Baptist Youth Fellowship meetings. After our meetings, we would have a Sip and Sing before going home. I had the use of our family car, so I would take up to five kids home. Kathy always made sure Florma sat next to me, and since she lived the farthest away, naturally, she was the last to get home.

After taking her home for about a year, I decided that she had all the qualities that I could ever ask for in a wife. She was intelligent with a good business head on her shoulders, an accomplished musician-piano and organ, and a very good student. In high school, she had all A's except for one B.

On the world's scale, Florma was not a ten; however, on my scale, she would be at least a fifteen. She was not a blond, air-headed bimbo with an hourglass figure but on their scale, still a good solid nine. She had developed many qualities way beyond her years. Very attractive with her auburn hair and hazel eyes, Florma was liked by everyone.

COLLECTIONS OF THE HEART

I decided that I wanted her to be my wife two years before we ever had a date. She was from May to Sept., older than me, but a year ahead of me in school. I was a year behind because I lost a year in the first grade. I was ready to start the fourth school in the second state before the end of the first semester, so the teacher said, "Stay home and start next year. You have lost too much."

In the "40's," it was common for a girl to date a boy older or ahead of her in school but rarely a boy behind her, so I bid my time. I did do a lot of praying, asking God for her hand in marriage, and He gave her to me. After she graduated high school, we started dating and making plans for our life together. When I graduated, Uncle was breathing down my neck, so I enlisted in the USAF. We planned our marriage as soon as I received a discharge.

When observing her mother and how she was brought up at home, I decided that she would be a good mother and homemaker. Long before we were married, I told her, "Your mother is an excellent cook, and I expect you to be as good or better," and she was. She also had a good solid Christian background.

Upon graduation from Business College, two of her girlfriends ask her to come along while they took tests at Patton State Hospital for sectorial positions. Florma knew the lady giving the test, so she, for fun, also took it. She was hired and worked for the head of the business office. In Wichita, she worked in the accounting department on the reports for Olive Beech, CEO of Beech Aircraft

Co, in Santa Barbara. She worked for Security Pacific Bank, one day as a teller and then moved to the trust department handling stocks and bonds, and finally in Pomona for the manager of the city building department.

However, when I was sent to Mc Connell AFB, Wichita, Kansas, and I learned that my full tour of duty would be there, we decided to get married. We became one on 31 July 1954.

In 1961 we joined Bethany Baptist Church in Montclair, and she became Director of the Middler Department, which is the third and fourth grade. If you get one of us, you get both of us, if possible. Yes, I taught in this department, but it is really too young for me, so I was transferred to the high school and finally to the adult class. I also spent many years on the Deacon Board and/or head of the Finance Committee. Florma was also director of Vacation Bible School for one year.

She was mine, and I was her's until God took her home on 5 Dec. 2011. There has never a day gone by that I do not think about her. Friends have asked me, "Why don't you get married again?" and the simple answer to me is, we are still married, and just because she is in heaven and I am not there yet does not change a thing. I will find her when I get there, even if it takes a long time, but I have all eternity to do it.

COLLECTIONS OF THE HEART

BURDENS
By Cindy Tesar

Matthew 11:28 "Come to me, all you who are weary and burdened, and I will give you rest."

A sack of flour and a sack of sugar are small bundles to carry, yet, just standing in line for fifteen minutes with a fretful ten-pound baby on your hip can feel like bearing the weight of the world. We often choose to carry way more than needed.

The woman started her journey, young and fresh, upright. And choosing to tote the burdens, walked up and down the aisles loading her biodegradable bags. After paying the cashier, she stepped to a nearby bench to redistribute the merchandise in somewhat equal proportions. She hoisted the bags, one on each arm, and made her way home. The concerns of the day piled their awkward load on her mind. She had acted badly toward someone the day before. Regret brought moisture-laden clouds to the sky above. Shifting the bags once again, she stepped off the curb a bit hunched over. Block after block, curb after curb, step-up, step-down, the miles drudgingly disappeared in her wake. A short stop at the family park for a drink of water gave her the opportunity to regroup, refresh. The bench was in a shady spot near the play area.

COLLECTIONS OF THE HEART

Children climbed the monkey bars and flew high on swings with reckless abandon. Laughter arose like helium balloons and lifted her spirits. She exhaled a stale breath, and with a smile, took up her packages and continued her journey homeward. Sun now shafted through a break in the clouds. Beads of perspiration dotted her upper lip. She hunched now, under the burden of her yoke, not recalling the way to be so long. Her body felt like she'd aged thirty years in just one day. "Just a few more blocks," she muttered as her feet shuffled to move forward. Her efforts seemed hindered somehow, dragging anchor. Again, she thought of the careless words spoken in anger the day before and wished they could be called back inside her personal vial of poison and sealed for all time.

By now, the sacks were dragging against the ground. Strength was failing. Dust to dust, ashes to ashes, and so her biodegradable bags chose the most *gawdawful* time for departure. Cans of peas, beans, and corn tumbled to the walkway and rolled into the gutter. Apples bounced and skinned their knees. The sacks of flour and sugar split and splattered into a replica of the Caribbean coastline. Right there in the midst of it all she dropped to her knees and cried, "Lawd'a mercy!"

(Now, you don't usually hear that kind of language unless you're from the south, seated before a plate of hot biscuits and gravy and ready to commit a felony against your diet.)

Just like that, Mercy rushed to her aid, helped her to her feet, and seated her in the cool air conditioning of the waiting vehicle. Gathering up the groceries and depositing them in the back seat, she spoke:

"I've been following you just waiting for you to cry my name."

A tear trickled down the woman's cheek, touched by such tenderness.

"If I'd a known that I would'a asked sooner!" And, embarrassed by her own stupidity, she hid her face in her hands. "When I get home, I have a phone call to make, an apology to deliver, and a story to tell. Mercy!"

"Indeed!"

CLOSE ENCOUNTERS OF THE BIRD KIND
by Cindy Tesar

My heart was overwhelmed with care as I kept vigil at mom's bedside, where she hovered on the edge of eternity. Brain cancer incapacitated her to the point of 24/7 care at home according to her wishes. One of the duty nurses arrived to relieve me just before the breaking point of emotions, duty, and energy. Needing escape, I grabbed the remainder of a huge bag of Price Club popcorn and headed to a little lagoon in Playa Del Rey just a few miles from her house. I walked barefooted through the mix of sand and grass to the edge of the water where ducks were leisurely paddling. I dug deep into the bag and scattered scoops of popped yellow kernels atop the water. The curious coots checked out my offering and swam away. Mallards and their plainer mates could not be bothered. In my rejection, I took a seat at a nearby bench and shoved a handful into my mouth.

The air smelled of ocean, and I was revived in spirit *by* the Spirit. A pigeon landed at my feet. His iridescent neck dazzled in the sunlight. Dropping feed in front of him, I finally found a taker. He was soon joined by another and another. I scooped out two fists full of corn and offered them openhandedly. Within seconds a pigeon landed on my wrist and then more perched along my arms like birds on a wire. All eagerly clung as I dipped into the bag over and over to replenish the supply. Overhead, seagulls arrived screeching for their fair share. I flung popcorn into the air, which they caught before it could hit the ground. Amid this unrehearsed bird carnival, I thought of the corn as my cares. God had graciously sent his feathered messengers to consume and carry

them all away. My unburdened heart could return home once again to keep watch.

1 Peter 5:7 NLT "Give all your worries and cares to God, for he cares about you."

CRYSTAL THE UNICORN
by Dennis Knotts

Once there was a herd of unicorn that lived in the last magical forest in the world. One by one, the power of other woodlands had been broken, stolen, or faded until only this one remained. As each unicorn was driven from their place when the enchantment was lost, they wandered the world, searching for a new unicorn forest. This was how they all came to live in this place.

It was not uncommon for two or maybe three unicorns to live in the same forest; however, for thirty of them to be found in the same place was unique.

There had been some problems with this since unicorns do enjoy their privacy. It was difficult to move through the forest without stumbling onto the others. Careful rules had to be laid down to ensure that each unicorn could be left alone.

One day, into these woods came another unicorn. She was different from the others. In place of the spiral gold or silver horns the other unicorns displayed; she bore a sleek transparent saber.

It did not spiral like the other horns. It was not as thick as a traditional horn but delicate in appearance, and this made her afraid to use her horn as others did, for fear it might break. It looked, for the world, like a glass sliver instead of an actual unicorn horn.

The fact that she was so different caused a great deal of concern with the others. The unicorns take pride in their horns. It is by the horn that the origin and age of the unicorn are recorded. Those who came from the east had silver ones. Those who came from the western shores had gold. The number of spirals on the horn told how old they were—one spiral for each century. There was no way to tell from where this unicorn came, nor how old she was. It became a difficult thing to place her in the community and to grant her the rights of the older unicorns.

It was with great reluctance that they allowed her to stay. Finally, it was decided that she would stay at the north end of the forest. It was normally wetter than the other parts and a little colder due to the north winds cutting into the woods. The trees kept the cold and rain out more to the south, so this was where the other unicorns would stay. Because the north was not pleasant, it was decided that this was where the newcomer would stay. It would have been a different story if she had been normal, and they could have told her age and given her legal status, but she was an outcast. Sadly, Crystal took her place. It was not as nice as her old forest, but a least it was miraculous and enchanted.

She vowed that she would make the best of it.

COLLECTIONS OF THE HEART

To *"make the best of it,"* Crystal had to do something none of the other unicorns had ever done. She worked. In their unicorn forests, they had been the rulers. All the other animals would bring food and prepare shelters for the unicorns because as long as the unicorns were in the forest, the animals were safe from hunters. Therefore, the animals went to great lengths to keep their unicorns happy. Perhaps this was what had made them so demanding and gave them such a few social graces. They had always gotten their way. This made it difficult at first when they all came together. They had to accept the idea of being equal with other unicorns. It was unheard of!

Finally, it was decided that a ranking system would be used. Those who were older had greater rights. When two were the same age, the gold would have greater rights than the silver. If two of the same color had the same age – which had never happened to date; then it would have to be decided between them who had the greater rights. It was not sure if the longer horn would gain power or the stronger. If the stronger was to rule, then the terror of a battle between unicorns would possibly take place.

As it was, Crystal was the lowest of the low. The other unicorns had brought their servant animals with them. Those in greater positions could take them for their own needs. When Crystal joined the community, her servants were taken by those over her. Now she found herself in the most unpleasant part of the forest, working on her own to provide meals and shelter for herself.

It would be untrue to say she accepted her fate with stoic resolve. For the first few weeks, she gave serious thought to leaving in the hope of finding another blessed forest. However, she had traveled so long and learned from the other unicorns who came from all over the world that magical forests were not to be found. When she finally came to accept that this was the last empowered woodland, she bemoaned her fate.

There were no other unicorns to complain to since they stayed in their warm, dry parts of the forest. Nor were there any animals, except an occasional migrating bird. Crystal soon developed the habit of talking to herself, and that was how she discovered her home.

"I wish I had someone to help me," she moaned to no one in particular.

"*Help me*," came a voice. A unicorn is normally too concerned with itself to risk danger for someone else. The only reason unicorns kept their animals safe from hunters was because they needed the workers. To be honest, unicorns had become very selfish creatures. When Crystal heard the voice, she startled. She had not heard another voice for so long, but this one sounded familiar. She perked her ears and waited for another cry. When none came, Crystal felt a little relieved. She did not dare use her horn in battle. If it were to break, she would be less than a unicorn. She would have to serve others or leave the forest.

I'm glad that's over with," she muttered. Her mind had been torn between giving help to someone and having them become her servant or having to fight and risk losing her horn. It was a relief

"*Over with*," came the voice again.

"Hello!" called Crystal, looking around.

"*Hello!*" called the voice.

"Come out so that I can meet you," she cried.

"*Meet you*," was all the vice answered.

Crystal wasn't sure if the voice was mocking her, questioning her, or only playing. It had come enough times for her to estimate that whoever was speaking was coming from behind the falls. She moved carefully along the shore, taking care not to make a sound. She worked her way along the face of the cliff so she could see behind the waterfall. No one was there.

She remembered stories told to her by others of invisible creatures. She felt the hairs on the back of her neck bristle. It was not common for unicorns to feel fear because their animals would fight for them; Crystal had no idea that kind of emotion could

COLLECTIONS OF THE HEART

make you so weak. She was, probably the first unicorn in several generations to know the sensation.

Her mouth was dry. Her tongue was dry, too, despite the spray from the waterfall. It was an unpleasant combination. She wasn't sure why, but she moved ahead. Perhaps it was due to her being alone for these long months and having to learn to do things for herself. It was slowly becoming a habit to get something on her own without asking.

At first, she would simply announce her need or problem, such as being hungry. In her forest, that was all she needed to send her servants running to tend her. When no one came, she would then take care of herself. Migrating birds stopped to visit, so she commanded them, but they ignored her and flew away. They were not trusting her to keep them safe. She asked them politely to get something she could not reach. Over time, she learned manners.

Now those years of doing for herself, or learning to ask, had brought her where no other unicorn had ever been; standing on the brink of fear. Her whole body trembled! Her knees were weak, and her ears and eyes played tricks on her. She wasn't sure why she had come back here, and she could never explain the motive. She now was at the falls; the cliff jutting out.

"Hello," she managed to blurt.

"*Hello,*" came the response. Still, no one was there. Fear begged her to turn and run. The old Crystal would have done that, but something urged her on.

"Is anyone there?"

"*Is anyone there?*"

"Yes!"

"*Yes!*"

The voice was mocking her. It would repeat everything she said. Anger came over Crystal. She pushed the fear away, and walked on.

"Come out!'

"*Come out!*"

As Crystal rounded the edge of the cliff, she found the source of her mocking voice! A vast cave was behind the falls, not visible to her until she dared to walk around and get wet.

"So this is an echo," she said to herself. It was her own voice. A migrating bird had mentioned it to her once, but she refused to believe someone's own voice could talk to them, but here it was.

Crystal smiled—something she had not done for a long time. She had now done something that made her feel good about herself. Not that she had found the only cave in the forest, something all the other unicorns would envy her for, but she had faced her fears. She experienced a NEW feeling. No other unicorn had recognized this feeling. It was pride. Not the kind of pride that is bad. All unicorns knew a bad pride – when you think you are great and expect others to treat you that way. No, the kind of pride Crystal felt came from self-respect when you've done something hard and succeed. No, only Crystal, of all the unicorns, experienced this kind of pride.

The roar of the falls was deafening, and she was drenched from the spray. This was the only haven from it, and so she worked her way in. To her surprise, the cave made two sharp twists and all the spray and noise were blocked out. That would have left her in complete darkness, but there was an opening in the ceiling. High in the back, a light shone. No other unicorn could have asked for a better home. Even the highest of the unicorns in the forest lived in what was little more than a mud and stick hut built by the animals. This would make her the envy of all the others…no, if she told them about it, Fytar, the leader, would take it away for himself. She would keep it to herself.

This was another thing hard for a unicorn to have; humility. Normally a unicorn would boast. The standing in the community was everything in this forest. She would have the best but could not flaunt it in front of the others. She went outside to gather soft ferns that grew in abundance because of the spray from the falls. These would make a wonderful bed. She smiled when she realized the others had to use dry grass or leaves for their beds. For the first time, in a long time, she slept in complete satisfaction.

***

Unicorns are almost immortal. Not that they are gods— there is only One God, but they are more than mortal. In this sense, time has no meaning to them. There are two kinds of immortals. There is the kind who finds this timelessness a burden that wears them down. They stagnate because they have no purpose. They exist, but they do not live. The others enjoy their immortality because they have found some purpose.

The difference is that when life is only an attempt to satisfy itself, it becomes hollow. When one lives to satisfy the needs of others, life has a purpose. While other unicorns grew stagnant, Crystal began to become one of the OTHERS.

***

It happened on what was a rather normal day for Crystal. She had just finished her morning meal. It has been a simple meal of nuts and berries, with an apple for dessert. These foods were always available because of the energy of the forest. This is what made a forest magical. There was an energy in it.

COLLECTIONS OF THE HEART

Some suggested that such special forests still vibrated with the last note of the Song of Creation which the One God had sung to bring everything into being.

There was a unique symbiotic relationship in these forests between the plants and the unicorn. There was energy that no one could sense or feel; and therefore, no one could use. But unicorns were unique. Some suggested that it was their horn that had been tuned to the Song of Creation. They could feel the harmonics of creation vibrating ever so softly in the trees and plants. Their horns could capture this echo of creation and focus it. Just as the One God had sung all things into existence, a unicorn could use its horn to channel that energy into assisting creation of life in the forest.

This is why enchanted forests were slowly disappearing from the world. As the world moved further from its creation, the vibrations of the final note of the One God's song reverberated less and less. Where once it had been a symphony, now it was barely a whisper. In some forests – the younger forests, which were several generations removed from the actual song; it was barely a soft humming.

The unicorn needed this music. Their horns blended with the energy lingering in the blades of grass and leaves of trees, and thus, they could continue the miracle of creation a little longer.

COLLECTIONS OF THE HEART

Of course, no one understood how the magic worked – or why it worked. They had just come to notice that unicorns could make it work; and this is why animals served the unicorn in order to partake of this special blessing.

In forests where the Song of Creation still lingered, all fruits and berries and nuts produced all year round. This is how a unicorn could know that it had wandered into an enchanted forest. Crystal had been able to find apples, peaches, oranges, and other sweet fruits if she wandered far enough throughout the forest. But when she did, she ran the risk of encroaching upon another unicorn's territory. That could create a serious breach, and the community would punish the offender – normally by reducing the size of the offender's own domain.

The issue of distance to find food had never been a problem for the other unicorns. Their servants would travel great distances, if need be, to provide for their unicorn. However, Crystal had no servants, and so she had been the one who had to travel the distances herself. It had recently dawned upon Crystal that she did not need to travel all that distance to find the delicacies she wanted. With her horn, she could bring the trees, fruits, berries, and nuts into her domain. This is what she was doing this morning.

As she was planting the seeds from her apple, a rabbit came scampering by. She had not seen a rabbit for a long time and was excited to visit.

COLLECTIONS OF THE HEART

"I can't stay long," explained the rabbit whose name was Boomer. "I have to find some apples for Sinark."

Crystal remembered Sinark. He was a young silver unicorn of seven centuries, low in rank. She remembered him because he had taken several of her servants, but Boomer wasn't one of them. He had been most demanding and harsh on those of less rank as someone of his low rank would have to be. Now he was sending servants into her part of the forest to find him some apples. He did not respect her in the least.

Crystal touched her horn to the ground where the seeds were planted. She enjoyed the life-giving power coursing through the horn. As she joined with the Song of Creation, her heart filled with joy, and a warm feeling came over her. She smiled and said,

"Stay a little while with me and visit. I know where there are some apples close-by." The stress on Boomer's face eased now that his mission was sure to be a success. He stopped and gave the latest gossip and news. What was the most distressing was that one of her old servants had died. It had been a hunter who came into the forest and killed her. Yenda was the name of the fox who had been so good to Crystal. When Boomer told the news, Crystal did what no other unicorn had done before; she wept. Boomer sat transfixed at the sight. Never had anything immortal done such a thing.

COLLECTIONS OF THE HEART

"Maybe being immortal makes one more or less so, depending on how you use your immortality," was all that Crystal would say.

All the time they spoke, Crystal kept Boomer's back toward the seeds she had planted. As the conversation continued, the tiny shoot broke through the ground. A tender stalk stretched high over Boomer and grew thicker. Leaves burst in an explosion of green and white apple blossoms that spread their petals toward the sun. Boomer's sensitive nose caught the fragrance. He paused, sniffed the air, and rose on his hind legs, nose wiggling and ears twitching. Soon the blossoms began to flutter to the ground, followed by the first crop of swollen juicy sweet apples.

Crystal laughed at Boomer's expression when he turned and saw the new tree behind him. The rabbit was surprised at the reaction from the unicorn. Laughter seemed such a natural thing to Crystal, and she could not understand Boomer's response.

"Why couldn't Sinark do that?" asked Boomer.

"I'm sure he could. Why don't you ask him?"

"No. If I did, he would fill with rage and spear me with his horn."

"Spear you with his horn? No unicorn would ever do that to a servant," insisted Crystal.

COLLECTIONS OF THE HEART

Boomer fell strangely quiet. Finally, he asked.

"May I please take these back to Sinark?"

"Of course, Boomer. That's why I grew the tree for you."

"For me?" asked the rabbit in disbelief. "No one has been that nice to me before. Do you treat all your servants this well?

"I have no servants," Crystal replied for the first time with no trace of anger or bitterness in her voice. In truth, the idea of treating another living thing in such a way seemed almost repulsive to her. It was a startling revelation.

"Could I be your servant?" asked Boomer.

Crystal smiled a warm smile that made Boomer sit up on his hind legs with expectation.

"If you were my servant, you could not stay." Boomer dropped to all four disappointed. "You see, I am the lowest of the low, and unicorn law would force me to give you to any other unicorn who would ask for you. However, if you want, you can be my friend. There is no unicorn law to forbid that."

Boomer's nose twitched excitedly. He stood up on his hind legs and said,

COLLECTIONS OF THE HEART

"I'd like that. I'd like that very much. I have to go now before Sinark gets angry. I'll come again tomorrow if you don't mind."

"Of course I don't mind. It's good to have a friend." With that, Crystal used her horn, careful not to break it while shaking off a few more apples from the tree for Boomer. When he had all he could carry, he hopped off toward the south, taking care not to bruise his treasure.

Boomer returned the next day, excited to visit with Crystal. She had been by herself for so long that she had forgotten all the proper manners her mother had taught her about the things that unicorns do and do not do. After several visits, Boomer realized he was late in returning. Crystal told him to climb on her back, and she carried him like the wind to the outskirts of Sinark's territory.

"*Not a proper thing at all!*" was what her mother had said many years ago when she dared to let a bird rest on her head. "*Image*" was all-important to the unicorn.

It was hard to keep such a secret from the other servants. Slowly the number of visitors who came to see Crystal grew. She would do what she could to make their tasks easier. She let them take from her storehouse of nuts, or she called forth berries. It was probably the most pleasant time of her life until that one day.

COLLECTIONS OF THE HEART

***

Boomer was late for his visit. Crystal became worried about him; first of all, because hunters had dared to come into these blessed woods and kill Yenda, and second because Sinark had not protected his servants. Lastly, the look of fear and inner turmoil on Boomer's face when he fell silent at her protest of the young unicorn striking a servant with his horn caused her to worry for her friend.

She was half-way to Sinark's territory when a squirrel by the name of Squint popped up on a branch before her.

"Don't go! Don't go!" his shrill voice chirped.

"Squint! What's the matter? Your tail is frizzed."

"Don't go. Boomer's in trouble. Sinark found out about you. Boomer is being punished. Don't go."

"I must go. Squint. Boomer is my friend, just like you."

"Boomer wants you to stay away. He does not want you to see him."

"Squint! The truth. What happened?"

"Sinark overheard Boomer talking when he mentioned your name. He flew into a rage, held him down with his hoof, and used his horn to cut off Boomer's tail. Boomer's ashamed now."

COLLECTIONS OF THE HEART

Crystal understood. Each animal was given a trait by their Maker. It was a trait each animal would take pride in. Just as the unicorn took pride in their horn; so a rabbit took pride in his tail. Crystal felt anger rise within her. She darted past the chattering squirrel, who jumped from branch to branch, trying to catch her, but she had the fire in her eyes.

"Sinark!" she shouted as she broke into the clearing. The young unicorn startled in shock. As he saw Crystal, his nostrils flared, he rose on his hind legs and pawed the air. The indignity of another unicorn daring to enter his territory in such a way! He lowered his horn and charged.

Crystal gave no thought for her safety, but she knew her horn was no match for the Silver. She waited for the right moment and then stepped aside. Sinark's horn pierced deep into the beech tree and held fast. Try as he might, Sinark could not work his horn free. The more he pulled, the tighter it grew.

"Help me!" he called to his servants. They all stepped back. It wasn't fear that kept them away, for they knew Crystal would not harm them. When Sinark finally realized his helpless position, he called out, "I yield!"

According to unicorn law, Crystal had proven she held a rank higher than Sinark's. She was obligated to release him, but Crystal had long been away from proper unicorn society.

COLLECTIONS OF THE HEART

"You dared clip a rabbit's tail?" she shouted. "I have a good mind to snap your horn and leave it embedded in that tree. You are not fit to be a unicorn."

Fear filled Sinark's heart, and he began to cry out, "Help me, unicorns; Help me!"

Within moments the other unicorns had entered the clearing. Fytar, the oldest of the clan, stepped forward and spoke, "Release him, Crystal. That is the Law of the Unicorns."

"It might be your law, but it is not mine!" she shouted. Her entire frame quivered with anger. "I live by the Ancient Law of the Unicorns. I claim his horn as is my right of battle."

"Battle?" snorted the ancient one.

"Yes, Sinark attacked me. That is how he came into this position."

"Is this true?" asked Fytar.

"Not true! Not true! She tricked me. She tricked me."

The servants all began to shout even though it was a violation of the unicorn law, "He lies! He lies!"

"He dares to lie to the Leader?" the ancient unicorn stammered in disbelief. "Take his horn, Crystal. He is not fit to be a unicorn."

COLLECTIONS OF THE HEART

Sinark began screaming for mercy. Begging for his horn as Crystal came at him. When she was only a few inches away, she hissed at him, "A deal, Sinark."

"*A deal*? What kind of deal?"

"Your servants for your horn."

"Give my servants to you? You must be insane. A unicorn without a servant is worthless. You know that."

"I know more than you give me credit for. A unicorn without a servant might be worthless, but a unicorn without a horn is no unicorn at all." She raised her hoof to snap the horn.

"Wait! Wait!" Take them; they're yours."

Crystal turned toward the herd. "They are mine by right of battle. According to the Ancient Law, no one may take them from me."

"They are faithless servants," Fytar declared. "No respectable unicorn would have them."

"They are loyal friends, and I am proud to claim them." She motioned for the servants to follow her as she headed back to her part of the woods.

"Are you not going to free me?" whined Sinark.

COLLECTIONS OF THE HEART

"When I feel you are ready. Until then, trust your friends to care for you and bring you food and water. You can try to free yourself if you wish, but you might snap your horn." Crystal left the clearing.

She asked some birds to stop and check on Sinark, and when he had not been freed after two days, she asked the beaver to chew through the tree trunk so Sinark could get free. The young unicorn was thirsty and hungry, weak from his experience, but even more so, his heart burned with anger because the beaver had forced him to say *"please"* before he would free him. A few weeks later, Sinark left the forest in disgrace.

The first thing Crystal did with her new servants was to set them free. She found that it was more satisfying to have people help you and work with you because they wanted to, not because they were forced to. Her second act was to call Boomer into the circle.

The rabbit was excited to be free of Sinark but embarrassed to be brought forth into public without a tail. Crystal calmed her friend. "Do you know the legend of our horn?"

"It's what makes you immortal," Boomer replied with confidence.

"Oh, it's more than that! Remember the apple tree I grew?"

COLLECTIONS OF THE HEART

"Yes…" Boomer replied, letting his voice trail off as if trying to figure out where this conversation was leading.

"Turn around." She instructed her friend. The rabbit was obedient and turned so his back was toward Crystal. She lowered her head, so her horn touched where his tail used to be.

"That tickles!" he giggled and squirmed. The other animals gasped in surprise. Boomer looked around to see what everyone was looking at. There, where it had always been, was a new tail!

***

As most stories go *"and they lived happily ever after,"* so this story continued. But many times, the *"happily ever after"* is only a bridge between one story and another. So it is with this.

Several years passed, and even though the older unicorns kept a closer eye on Crystal, the incident with Sinark was soon pushed out of their memories. Unicorns, being immortal, do not forget, but they can choose to remove information from their minds until they need it again. They did so until years later…

***

It was a warm day for this time of year. The leaves never drop from the trees of a blessed forest, but they do turn color with the seasons. So it was that the leaves had gone into a hibernation of red and gold only a few weeks before. But now it was a warm late spring day as the leaves began to turn green once more. The sky was covered with a dark cloud formation that swirled with the stench of death.

"Smoke!" Boomer shouted. He was no longer the young rabbit in search of adventure. Now he had a wife and family to care for; and he remembered the fires of long ago that drove them from their first home and into the protected woods.

"Smoke?" questioned Crystal munching an apple as it hung on the tree.

"It comes from fire," Boomer added, beginning a nervous twitch with his nose. The rabbit was sure that should have given his friend the entire picture to realize the danger they were in, but unicorns had lived by the power of the Song of Creation and had little need of knowledge of fire except in their legends.

"When something burns," Boomer added. "It's like when lightning strikes a tree, and it explodes, and all its pieces turn from wood into a soft powder called *ash*. As it does, the pieces give off great heat and light, and a black cloud called smoke."

"So, you are saying that lightning has struck a tree near-by? It is strange because lightning does not strike in a unicorn forest."

Lightning is just one way fire is made. Mankind knows how to make fires without lightning. He strikes stones together or rubs sticks. But when there is fire, it is not safe. I doubt if even an immortal could survive a fire."

Somewhere in the back of Crystal's mind, the concept of fire was tugging at a memory she had stored away centuries ago. Rather than opening the door and examining the memory, Crystal chose to accept what Boomer had said.

"Then let's go and see this wonder and see if it is a threat to our home and friends."

"One does not go to a fire. You run from a fire."

"Perhaps, but first, I must make sure…" Crystal's comment was cut short by a sound few had heard before, but once it had been heard, it haunted their memories forever. It was the scream of a unicorn in pain. Crystal broke into a full gallop, slipping between trees with a grace that few could imagine. Even as the scream of the lead unicorn echoed more intense. Crystal broke into the glen.

"Fytar!" she cried.

The ancient steed raised his tear-filled eyes. The pain etched on his brow, where blood trickled down. The scar, which was once his horn, told the story. Behind him stood,

"Glaymot!"

The door to the memory she had ignored now burst open unbidden. Small unicorns had been hushed into silence with tales of Glaymot the dragon. His title had been *Unicorn-Slayer* for all the tales told of how his burning breath brought death to the early unicorns. He had been unseen for centuries, many believed him dead, and most prayed he had been only a legend. The black-red scales of their ancient foe glistened as light from the burning brush danced with each motion. The massive tail snapped, and trees were shattered.

Crystal felt their pain, but it was nothing compared to the pain of the Old One. He had mellowed over the years. Crystal would mourn his passing. Although not mortally wounded, his horn was gone and so was his immortality.

A figure moved in the shadows of the great dragon. Another unicorn without its horn, but this one was not in pain. This one gloated.

"Sinark!" hissed Crystal. "Your horn?"

"A small price to pay for this day," the stallion spat. He shook his mane. The scar was old, and Crystal's eyes caught the silver horn adorning the brow of the ancient foe. "Yes, unicorn, Glaymot sports a unicorn horn, my horn. The price I paid for his aid. He now has the same immortality as the unicorns. The soon-to-be-extinct unicorns."

COLLECTIONS OF THE HEART

Crystal looked around her. Several unicorns were scattered around the glen. Some were bleeding, but all still had their horns. Only Fytar had been so damaged.

"No, we have not taken their horns, yet;" Sinark snarled. "But we will. I wanted you to stand by, helpless to stop us."

"I will have my revenge for those many battles I lost and the wounds that drove me deep into the earth," Glaymot bellowed. His hind right foot pawed the earth and ripped grass and roots from their bed.

"That is where I found him," Sinark continued the tale. "I used my horn to heal him and now together we will destroy the last of your race, then we will take our pleasure with you."

Crystal noticed the other unicorns had come to the glen in response to Fytar's cry of pain. They stood in terror. Several called for their servants to save them. Even as she watched, three wolves charged Glaymot to protect their unicorns. The belch of flames ended their cries.

"Enough!" shouted Crystal. The other unicorns had grown docile. They did not act. Without orders from Fytar, who now collapsed to the ground in a state of shock, the herd had no direction. Crystal saw only one hope for them.

COLLECTIONS OF THE HEART

"Follow me!" she cried and led the unicorns into her part of the woods. Several of the servants fled for their lives. Behind them, the cries of Sinark and the roar of Glaymot filled the forest. The dragon began to follow. The ground quaked, the trees shook. Crystal could feel the death of numerous trees and brush as the dragon crushed them under his weight. As the unicorns were swifter, Crystal brought them to her falls before the dragon could reach them.

"Behind the falls! Glaymot can't use his breath. The opening will keep him out." The unicorns threaded behind the spray and gasped in amazement when they found the cave. The servants who had stayed with their unicorns scurried to make room for their masters.

"What about Fytar and the others?" called Boomer as he motioned Crystal's friends into the cave.

"If Sinark hates me enough to surrender his horn, he hates me enough to forget about them and come after us."

"What can we do?" bemoaned Jendar. "The food will not last. We must leave sooner or later." The truth dawned on Crystal. Although the cave would keep them safe, it was only a prison so long as the dragon remained.

"We must beat Glaymot!" she cried. The unicorns gasped at Crystal's suggestion.

"We are not warriors! Our horns cannot pierce his scales. There is no way."

"Then I must find one. Perhaps if I meet him alone, Sinark will give up and leave. He doesn't know you are in the cave. He might think you have left the forest."

"You won't go alone," insisted Boomer as he and the other friends joined the unicorn.

"Your horn will snap. What chance does your horn stand when gold and silver did not?" shouted Hessler in near panic.

"Look! This isn't easy for me to do. I'm going to do it. I have to do it. Don't make it any more difficult." Crystal cleared the cave and the falls just before Glaymot tore down the trees before the pond.

Several birds dove for Glaymot's eyes, clawing them. The dragon raged and bellowed fire and smoke into the air; the birds barely escaped the heat. Two beavers had gnawed through a tree, so it fell on Glaymot, but the dragon caught it as it fell and snapped it like a twig. When the dragon nearly crushed Boomer's family with the branches, Crystal called out,

"Enough! This is my battle. Go back to your families. I will meet him alone." Crystal rose on her hind hooves. Glaymot spewed fire as she rose. She barely escaped the blast by rolling onto her back. As she got to her feet another branch crashed next to her. Wherever Crystal moved, Glaymot blocked her. Through it all Sinark cried out,

"Don't let her escape. Make her use her horn. Make her use her horn."

Finally, Crystal had no choice. She was surrounded by broken trees, rocks, or fire. The unicorns had long ago learned they could not pierce Glaymot's scales with their horns. Many great and noble steeds had sacrificed their horns so others could escape. Crystal had little hope for her sliver of glass, but it was all she had left. She lowered her head and charged.

Glaymot had faced the unicorns many times before. He did not fear their puny horns. His pride was so great that he rose on his hind haunches, exposing his belly in defiance to the slender horn. Sinark began to laugh with delight.

The laughter was cut short by the shriek of pain. It was not the pain-cry of a unicorn losing its horn as all expected Crystal to do. It was the scream of Glaymot. Blood sprayed from his belly where Crystal's horn had torn a wide gash. He fell over from the pain and before he could move his massive frame, Crystal spun around and drove her horn into his chest.

Glaymot bellowed as his heart was pierced by the sliver. His bulk shivered in death; and then the eyes of the dragon closed forever, a foul last belch of smoke announcing his death. But as he rolled over, his tail snapped and thrashed wildly, crushing Sinark under its weight.

The other unicorns came from the cave cheering. The animals returned from their hiding places. Crystal led the crowd back to where Fytar and the others lay.

"Tend to their wounds!" Crystal shouted.

The unicorns moved from one injured to another, touching their wounds with their horns and healing them while Crystal cared for Fytar.

"You ARE the unicorn of prophecy," he muttered.

"What are you talking about?" asked Crystal helping him back to his feet. "What prophecy?"

"There is a legend given to the first herd of unicorns. I am the last of the herd. We have not spoken of it for fear we might alter it. There is one who was to come whose horn would not be of silver or gold, but diamond. Strong enough to pierce even Glaymot's hide."

But why did you treat me so poorly when I came if you knew?"

"I did not know. There had been others, but they were not the ones. Only one would have the true heart of the first unicorns.

COLLECTIONS OF THE HEART

You needed to refine that heart, to develop that inner strength. When you came, your horn was only glass; but the trials that forged your spirit hardened your horn into what it could be."

"But how can we be sure?" asked Crystal.

"There is only one way to tell. Touch your horn to the scar on my brow."

Crystal did as the Old One requested. A glow of light danced down her horn and suddenly a spark flashed from Fytar's wound. Out of its glow, a new horn appeared as bright gold and as long as the first.

"Only the unicorn of the prophecy can restore a unicorn's horn. When you threatened Sinark's horn I was unsure. When you spared him I began to wonder. Now I know." Fytar lowered his head and touched his horn to the ground before Crystal. It was the sign of submission among the unicorns, but it has been centuries since it had been done. All the others followed the example.

"You are now the new leader of the unicorns. What do you desire?"

"I desire peace for our people. I desire freedom for the servants, and a chance for us to grow as we were meant to be." Several grumbled when Crystal mentioned giving up their servants, but Fytar's stern eyes quieted them. The animals scurried away, free for the first time in their lives. They would return later to test the freedom, but for now, most were afraid they would lose it.

With servants gone, the unicorns had to learn to care for themselves. They had to learn those magic words seldom heard before in the blessed forest: *"Please"* and *"Thank you."*

The unicorns grew in social graces and once more became the noble creatures that they had been in the days of the Garden of Eden. It was with this nobility and purity that they were able to regain what made forests special once again. And so, it was truly possible for them all to live *"happily ever after."*

©Copyright 1993, Dennis Knotts

El Vale De La Muerte
(The Valley of Death)

by Jim Hutcheson

We were flying at two thousand feet, looking at the beautiful green canopy of the Amazon jungle. Our flight plan was now following the Ucayali River, a tributary of the Amazon. Several times, along the river, we noticed small clearings with native villages and wisps of smoke from cooking fires and men in dugout canoes fishing.

Jim Johnson, an Ex-Navy Seal and a helicopter pilot, has a degree in Geology from the "University of California," Albert Hanson, former NASA satellite image interpreter's degree is in Geology from the "University of Michigan," Juan Ortega, Ex-Army Major's field is Linguistics and has a geology degree from "Stanford University," and me, Harvey Brant, Ex-Army Captain, Explosives-Ordnance Demolition expert, has a geology degree from the "University of Arizona."

Jim called out over the choppers intercom as we were approaching, "Pucallpa, Peru, Guys, take a good look. This may be the last time you see civilization for the next three months." It was about dusk when we parked the chopper close to an old DC-3 which had the rest of our gear on board.

After checking in at the local hotel, we decided to see a little of the city and pick up some "snake bite medicine," three bottles of Tequila, four bottles of Jack Daniel's, and a bottle of rum.

The next morning while we loaded gear aboard the chopper, Juan filed our flight plan and cleared up any last-minute details with the local authorities. Returning, he said that Paco Ruiz, from the airport, said, "Don't go there. People who go there don't come back. Sometimes we find their bones and equipment. Bad place." Smiling, we lifted off and headed for the valley anyway.

Al studied many satellite images and identified several possible locations for our base camp. Site requirements are: chopper accessible, fairly level, and near a spring or stream for water. We will be about 75 miles from Pucallpa in a remote area of the foothills of the Andes. The valley is about a mile wide and four miles long, with the mountains rising abruptly on three sides.

Flight time from Pucallpa is about 45 minutes. There is lush green vegetation on the valley floor, not too dense, and mountain foliage on the hills. This would be a hunter's paradise. Flying around the area looking at the sites Juan picked, his number two looked the best.

COLLECTIONS OF THE HEART

Jim circled the site a couple of times and then set her down nice and easy. Over the chopper's intercom, he said, "Well, guys, this is your new home for the next three months. How do you like it?"

After unloading our supplies, Jim and Juan flew back to Pucallpa for more of our equipment. Jim figured it should take about three trips to get all our equipment. Meanwhile, Al and I cleared the landing area, erected our sleeping tent, an easy up and scouted the immediate area.

About thirty yards southeast of our camp, just over a small ridge, was a spring. Surveying the spring, I said to Al, "Don't go near here. It looks like bad water; there are too many dead things around it. I need to analyze this before we touch any of this water."

On the other side of the camp, just a short way in a gully, was a nice creek. I'll analyze this water before we use it. We could now hear the chopper coming with our gear, so we headed for the landing site. Hurriedly we offloaded our supplies, and Jim and Juan flew back for another load. They should be back well before dusk.

While they were gone, Al and I finished erecting tents for our living quarters, relaxing area, and kitchen and set up our solar power generating system for running our equipment, lights, and battery recharging system. For safety's sake, we broke out and

COLLECTIONS OF THE HEART

loaded our AK47's and strapped on sidearms. You never know what the night will bring.

When the chopper came into view, we had a little over an hour of light left before nightfall. Unloading the chopper and securing everything for the night, we fixed dinner and got ready for our first night's rest. It was a new moon night very dark, which made the stars seem very bright. At first, the night sounds seemed similar to what we have experienced many times. However, about an hour 2245, there was what sounded like a loud woman screaming close by. Juan hollered, "What was that?" Jim replied, "I don't know, but we better be ready for whatever!" Needless to say, we didn't get a lot of sleep that night.

Along about sunup, since we were wide awake, Jim and Juan headed to Pucallpa for our last load of equipment. Meanwhile, Al and I scouted the area looking for wildlife and tracks. Some of the birds and small animals were beautiful, interesting, and different. We saw parrots, macaws, toucans, and others that I did not recognize, all with brilliant white, red, yellow, orange, green, blue, and black plumage. Animals were the hairy armadillos, capybaras, vicunas, and blacktail deer.

In a small tree, near the stream, on a branch about four feet from the ground, there was a Green Tree Boa about five and one half feet long eyeing a small rabbit waiting for it to get into range for a nice meal. I picked up a rock and threw it, hitting the branch just

COLLECTIONS OF THE HEART

above the snake. Startled, the snake jumped from the tree and quickly slithered away. The rabbit ran in a different direction, thus saving its life for another day.

We did not find anything that would account for the scream. We had our geologist picks with us, so we brought back some ore samples. Some samples were from igneous outcroppings and others from sedimentary deposits.

We were about a quarter mile from the camp when we heard faint chopper noise, so we hurried to the landing site arriving just before the chopper. All of our equipment was here now, so we started our field lab set up.

Using his satellite maps, Al has partitioned the area into sixty-four sections. We should be able to do one per day with extra time for some in-depth exploration. Each section is roughly one quarter mile square.

The Andes Mountains were formed when the Pacific Plate and the South American plate came together, and one slipped over the other. Then pressure from the magma forced the cooler top surface up, forming the mountains. In this process, the heat and the force of the magma formed rare earth elements. Rare-earth that have been eroded from exposed rocks have been collected in placer deposits. Other rare-earth will be in veins of other ores. The periodic table lists seventeen rare earth elements, and you use some of them in your home every day.

After analyzing the water from the spring and the creek, I told the guys, "Stay away from the spring. That water is very toxic. Put some electrodes in it, and you could use it for a battery. The creek is safe for drinking as long as it is filtered." The rest of the day was used, finishing setting up our preliminary field analyst lab.

Early the next morning, we thoroughly inspected and mapped section one, taking samples from outcroppings. We also set up geophones and made a seismic reading of the subsurface terrain. From these samples and readings, we should locate placer deposits, igneous and plutonic intrusions, and metamorphic zones that contain rare-earth. In section one, we found a few traces but nothing of ore grade quality. By checkerboarding the sections, we will be able to eliminate unproductive areas quicker.

The seventh section is beginning to look more promising. Outcropping samples are showing good streaks of Cerium and Neodymium. When we analyzed the seismic readings, they indicated a small placer deposit in a streambed. This placer deposit does not warrant mining, but it does denote the need for further exploration. The mountains at this point are rising more abruptly and are showing magma or lava flows and fumaroles. These cliffs are very pockmarked with shallow caves. While I was examining the mouth of one of these caves, suddenly ten thousand bats flew at me. These are fruit-eating bats that do not present a threat.

Section fifty-one and small parts of thirty-six and fifty-two are covered by a small lake. Approaching the lake, we saw some trees and waterfowl near one edge. Everything looked peaceful, but we soon encountered an animal I have never seen before. It had a mouth like a gator and a body and legs much longer, claws, and hide like a monitor lizard. I do not want to argue with this critter.

While examining sections forty-six through forty-eight and sixty-two through sixty-four, our search hit pay dirt. Outcroppings were rich in rare earth ores, and the seismic data indicated a large vein running back under the cliff at the head of the canyon.

Our biggest surprise, however, was found at the base of the cliff, a pile of debris consisting of human and animal bones, shredded cloth, boots, hunting gear, including a rifle with a barrel bent nearly ninety degrees. While searching through this pile, we sensed someone or something watching or tracking us.

As we were leaving, I looked at the face of the cliff and up about seventy feet, I saw a large cave opening and in it was a very large creature. It stood on two feet like a man, had long arms like an ape, its body was covered with long shaggy hair, and it was about twelve feet tall. It bellowed out a scream as we heard on our first night. This unnerved us, and we made a hasty retreat.

COLLECTIONS OF THE HEART

Just before dusk, we heard a scream again, only this time much closer. The creature was coming through our kitchen area, and pots and pans were flying everywhere. Grabbing our AK47's, we stopped it by firing about thirty rounds from twenty feet before it fell backward.

We hauled it away from camp a short distance and set up lights to illuminate the area all night. Tonight, we slept in four-hour shifts, with one eye open, keeping watch over the dead body for its mate or others to come and attack us or wild beasts to feast on the carcass. After breakfast, Jim and Juan flew to Pucallpa to report the incident to the proper authorities.

While Jim was servicing the chopper, Juan talked to Paco, telling him about the creature that attacked us. Paco's comments were, "Madre Mia, Mapinguari es Muerto. Gracias, Gracias, Gracias." Paco was thrilled that it or, as we call it in The United States, Big Foot or Sasquatch, was dead. It won't cannibalize any more people. Paco hopes that there aren't anymore.

We brought back all our equipment, loaded the DC-3, and prepared to return to the States. The authorities told us just to leave the body there and let the wild animals take care of it. They wanted nothing to do with it.

In our lab in Irvine, Ca. we have the equipment to make a more detailed analyst of the data we collected in the field. If this data indicates that this venture will be profitable, we will begin mining the rare-earth, cerium, and neodymium.

FPB-M 927

by Jim Hutcheson

Time: 0400 hours, Place: Dock on the Aung River. A thick fog swelled around the bare lamp at the end of the pier as the last of the stores put on board, and the companionway hoisted aboard.

Jack Garcia, Capt. of the "Quan-Tu, FPB-M 927", while looking from the bridge, toggled the intercom, "Deck crew, cast off the mooring lines." Turning to the helmsman, he said, "hard starboard rudder, port engine forward --steering."

The helmsman replied, "Aye sir." and the boat began to creep away from the pier. Our bow was now 20 meters from the pier, turning out into the channel.

When we had turned 135 deg., Capt Jack called out, "Helmsman, port engine forward ¼, starboard engine forward ¼. rudder amidships." We continued our turn but straightened out right down the channel. As we passed the light on the end of the pier, it's glow was eerie.

A little farther down the channel, we passed the submarine pens. Their big massive hulls silhouetted in the fog and dim light made them look menacing. Capt. Jack called out, "Radar, scan the channel for obstacles." Radar, "All clear, sir."

There were several fishing boats still tied to their wharves, getting ready to put out to sea for some early morning fishing. In the glow of their lights and the fog, they too were not very discernible. By now, we could feel and hear the slap of the running tide as it came up the channel. When we passed the light on the end of the jetty, there was just a slight glow in the Eastern horizon. Time 0515, Capt. Jack called out, "Helmsman, all engines forward ½." The boat began to pick up speed, and we were well on our way. We held our course for 2 hours and 45 min. at which time there was a course correction to 270 degrees true, and in another hour and 30 minutes, GPS told us we were entering the missile range.

Just then, the radio squawked, "Quan Tu this is Heilo squadron 17 over. Heilo squadron 17 this is the Quan Tu, over. Quan Tu, the

COLLECTIONS OF THE HEART

missile range has been swept,---it's clean--- target in place. Over and out."

Capt. Jack replied, "Thank you, Heilo 17, Out." Capt. Jack calls out, "Radar, sweep the range and give me a bearing, and range to the target."

"Aye, Sir." Radar, " Range---Clear, Bogey---Range---94 kilometers---Bearing---285 true."

Capt. Jack, "Helmsman, come about to 285 true."

"Aye Sir, 285 true."

The "Quan Tu" is a Yast class patrol boat. Displacement: 227 metric tons, Length: 47.3 meters, Beam: 6.9 meters, Propulsion: 2 GE turbine engines, Speed: 42 knots, Endurance: 3500+ kilometers, Crew: 3 officers, 18 enlisted personnel, Armament: 2- 50 caliber machine guns, 2- M240B machine guns, 1- 85mm deck canon, 4- FIM-92 Stinger SAMs and 4- MK-7 Brutis SAM/SSMs

An hour and a half later, Radar reports: "Bogey—Range--64 kilometers, Bearing--2 points off Starboard Bow."

Capt Jack toggles the intercom. "Attention all hands, prepare Port missile for launch. At the push of a button, the lid on the port missile coffin raises to launch position, and the blast door opens. There is "Brutis" gleaming in the now sunlit blue sky. Examining this beautiful white bird, we notice that this is a telemeter round. The telemeter is where the warhead normally is located. Brutis is about 12 feet long and 18 inches in diameter.

Capt. Jack, "Missileman, squawk telemetry, ID target, and set all systems 'go.'"

"Aye, Sir." Missile man, "Target squawked and IDed. All systems--go."

Capt. Jack, "Radar, how do you read?"

Radar, "Missile locked on target, range 52 kilometers, all systems go."

Capt. Jack on the intercom, "Attention all hands, Missile free, --- Missile free ready for launch." At this, the missile man inserts the firing key into the circuit turns the key, preparing the missile for launch. His hand is now near the firing switch, ready to launch the missile.

COLLECTIONS OF THE HEART

Capt. Jack, over the intercom, "Attention all hands. The missile will be launched on my count. 10---9---8---7---6---5---4---3---2---1, and there is the roar of Brutis as it passes right over the signal bridge of the Quan Tu on its way to the target. Capt. Jack, "Missileman, how do you read?"

"Looking good sir," Radar, "How do you read?"

The strobe lines on his scope indicate that the missile is locked onto the target. Radar, "looking good, sir."

Capt. Jack, "Helmsman, all engines flank speed, bearing ---285 true." Missile man, "Sir, preliminary TM data indicates a direct kill."

In about 45 minutes, we can see the target way off in the distance. Coming closer, the target, an old decommissioned Flecher class destroyer, is listing to the stern, --way too much to board. Pictures are taken of the starboard side where the missile entered and then of the port side where it exited. The kinetic energy of the missile left a much bigger hole in the port side, where it exited just below the waterline. The target is now listing so that the bow is now above the waterline.

Capt. Jack, "Helmsman, all engines ahead ½, bearing 85 true."

COLLECTIONS OF THE HEART

This takes us away from the target, and at about 500 meters, Capt. Jack calls out, "Helmsman, engines--steering, bearing 100 degrees. True, Gunny, man your canon. Fire when ready." Fire, the round goes just over the 0 Deck just forward of the superstructure. Gunny adjusts the gun down two clicks and left four clicks, fire. This round hit's the hull amidships. The next round hits just above the waterline.

By now, the target is sinking fast, stern first to "Davey Jones Locker" in 40 fathoms of water. We turn and head back to port. Capt. Jack toggles the intercom, "Well done men. Chief, run the broom up the yardarm. We have a clean sweep."

Tonight, the crew will celebrate, ---beer and babes.

Hard Rock Gold
by Jim Hutcheson

The Ransburg Mining district is in the chaparral-covered hills of the Mojave Desert just east of the southern end of the Sierra-Nevada Mountain Range. This is an area rich in minerals.

On Saturday the miners and their families usually go into Johannesburg California to shop and catch up on the news of the day. While the women shop the men gather at the Golden Nugget Saloon for a beer and companionship.

Billy Bob and Short Fuse were enjoying their beer when Slim came hurriedly through the door shouting,

"Have you boys seen what President Roooosevelt has done to us miners?"

Billy Bob interrupted saying, "Hold on Slim, it ain't that bad. He passed a law that say's, *before the 1st. of May 1933 we have to turn in all our gold coins, gold bullion, and gold certificates.* That don't mean that we can't mine for gold. We can still mine and take it to the assay office just like we always have."

As Short Fuse began to speak, Marg, Billy's wife hollered through the door, "Billy Bob, come on. Wee's got to get home. I have a lot to do."

Short Fuse continued, "Slim, you ain't got nothing to worry about. Just keep mining. It don't mean a thing."

Slim was an ex-German Army Sgt. who studied geology in Munich before the war. His mine near Red Mountain is called The Iron Cross.

Short Fuse's mine The Golden Poppy is in the Atolia area. Short Fuse earned his name when he lit a stick of dynamite, turned to leave and tripped. The dynamite exploded while he was a little too close, so now his hearing is bad and he has a lot of scars from the shards of quartz.

Billy Bob and Marg came out west from the panhandle of Texas during the dust bowl and staked their claim a mile from Ransburg. It's The Yellow Rose. Besides the mine, Billy Bob runs a stamp mill. Miners bring their ore to him to have it crushed to extract the gold from the quartz.

On the drive home, in their 1927 Reo, Billy Bob informed Marge that Slim has some ore to run through the mill that afternoon.

COLLECTIONS OF THE HEART

Arriving home, he helped Marge with her packages and then headed to the mill to get it ready. After the mill is prepped, he walked a short distance over to the mine, which is a horizontal shaft at about a 15 deg. decline into the side of the mountain. An ore car is sitting there ready to bring ore out of the mine. In the shade of the ore car, he noticed a sidewinder all coiled trying to stay cool away from the hot desert sun. Billy Bob grabbed a shovel, killed the sidewinder, and threw it over on the slag heap.

About that time, Billy Bob heard Slim's old Model A truck chugging up the hill to the stamp mill. Slim hollered "Billy Bob, let's get started." After loading the quartz into the mill feed, Billy started the old engine and you can hear it's clanking from a mile away. About 45 minutes later, Slim gathered the crushed quartz and headed for home. Back at his mine, Slim used a gold pan to separate the nuggets from the crushed quartz and then mercury to pick up the fine powder gold from the quartz sand.

Meanwhile, Billy Bob grabbed a star drill and hammer and headed into his mine. The mine head is in about 150 feet and this is where he is drilling holes to plant dynamite. Three holes have already been drilled and the fourth about three quarters finished. There are two holes on either side of the gold vein. When the last hole is completed, dynamite planted with short fuses tied together to a long fuse will burn for twenty seconds. This will allow him to be a safe distance away from the explosion.

Holding the end of the fuse in his hand, he looked around, listened intently, and then shouted three times, "**Fire In The Hole, Fire In The Hole, Fire In The Hole,**" lit the fuse and hurriedly walked to and through the mine entrance and stepped to one side out of the blast force field. There is a loud boom. Dust and small shards of quartz came rolling out of the mine entrance. When the dust settled, Billy turned and started towards the mine when he heard Marge call, "Billy, come on, it's time to eat."

Mining is hard work and Marge fixed a good supper, braised pork chops, mashed potatoes with pan gravy, green beans, and coffee. After the kitchen is cleaned, Marge and Billy relax by listening to the nightly news followed by *Fibber Mc Gee and Molly* and then *Gang Busters*.

Sunday morning, all decked out in their Sunday-go-to-meeting clothes, Billy Bob and Marge headed to the Community Church in Joeburg. Pastor Perkins was preaching from John 8: 1-11, "The God of All Comfort." After the service, several couples went to *Jennie's Café* for diner and socializing before returning home.

Monday morning right after breakfast, Billy Bob went up to the mine and loaded all the loosened quartz ore into his ore cart and rolled it to the stamp mill for processing. After crushing the quartz,

COLLECTIONS OF THE HEART

extracting the gold, and adding it to existing gold mined in the last two weeks he has 14 troy ounces of pure gold.

Turning this in at the "Assay Office" at $32.00/oz. made this a very profitable two weeks in the economy of 1933.

This is hard rock mining.

HIRAM ON THE HEIGHTS
by Cindy Tesar

From the time of his infancy, Hiram was a climber. There was not a crib, gate, or wall he couldn't climb. By age three, his reputation was notorious. Once he started school, he climbed atop every structure on the playground. He was *King of the Monkey Bars,* walking above the rungs where other kids hung by their fingers. He leaped, surefooted as a mountain goat to the top of the swing set and pretended to walk a tightrope across Niagara Falls.

The playground proctor nearly blew her brains out through her whistle, commanding Hiram, **"Get down from there!!!!"** *There* happened to mean the top of the equipment shed, the height of the swing set, top of the monkey bars, trees, the roof of the school, and every high wall. He simply could not help himself. Where there was anything that could be climbed, he was on top of it in a heartbeat. Clearly, something had to be done!

Hiram was a good, polite, and apt student in the classroom. He was not a bad boy, just someone who could not manage to control himself when the urge to climb came upon him. "I will climb to the heights! I will climb up to heaven!" His impulse was becoming a safety issue at school as other children tried to imitate his antics, fell, and hurt themselves. After repeated warnings to quit climbing, the principal talked to his parents. Mutually they decided he would be a good candidate for homeschool. Hiram's mom was a teacher. She was willing to instruct him and work to channel his impulse to climb. His father was a carpenter and could find work just about anywhere. They decided to move from the flatlands of Kansas to the Rocky Mountains of Colorado so that Hiram could practice his climbing in a more productive way.

The air was crisp and fresh in Colorado, where Hiram's father built a sturdy cabin in the woods just outside of town. They were nestled at the base of a mountain with various boulders and rock faces ideal for climbing. Though he thoroughly enjoyed learning about all the earth sciences and rock formations, daily Hiram would rush through his lessons so he could have the freedom to explore the great outdoors. The mountain became his playground.

Each year he grew stronger and safer as his parents equipped him with climbing shoes, ropes and anchors, harness, gloves, and a helmet. By the time he turned 16, he required only 4 hours of school and then took off for another 4 hours of climbing. He was dedicated to being the best. He always returned for dinner with a hearty appetite. It was a good thing that his father was an apt hunter and that his mother grew a great garden and kept a large flock of chickens for the boy certainly could eat! They were contented in their back-to-nature approach to life. It put roses in their cheeks and joy in their souls.

***

After a particularly productive morning of lessons on the eve of Hiram's 17th birthday, Ma made an early lunch and packed extra chicken and apples in Hiram's backpack. She cautioned him to return early as a storm was likely to hit their area before nightfall.

"Ma, don't worry, I'll come back just like I always do!"

Kids often trust that they will be fine without their parents' worry. He had everything he needed. His equipment was all in good working order, and Ma had made him take a jacket *just in case...*

She kissed him goodbye just as she always had, but something nagged at her right in the middle of her tummy. Perhaps it was the fried chicken and coleslaw she'd eaten at lunchtime. For a while, she just rubbed at the spot and waved to Hiram as he disappeared over the hill.

COLLECTIONS OF THE HEART

The mountain called to Hiram as he climbed. He believed it was whispering his name on the breezes that blew through the lower aspen trees.

"Hiram...Hiram?"

He reached for handholds and footings along the rocky face.

"I'm coming!" he called to the wind.

After about two hours of steady climbing, he needed to stop for a little bit of water and a hand full of his mom's special homemade trail mix. Resting against a boulder with firm footing behind a tree he looked out over a canyon. From his perch, he could spy range after range of icy peaks as hawks and eagles hang-glided on the currents of the wind. Such a glorious sight! It nearly took his breath away. He memorized the moment in his mind. What he didn't see from his vantage point was a bank of dark clouds scudding slowly into the area.

He began to climb just a little higher, avoiding some rotted branches and broken timber leftover from winters past. Suddenly, he hit a gravelly patch. His feet slipped, and they sent a skittering of shale: over the cliff. He grabbed a branch sticking out just above his head. *Whew! That was a close one!* He'd never encountered much in the way of troubles on the trail. Yes, he'd met up with a few snakes here and there and disturbed some creatures in their native habitats, but never had a fear of falling, really. He was Hiram, after all. *The Master Climber, King of the Mountain; Mighty Conqueror of the Heights!* In his estimation, he was unstoppable.

After his little self-pep talk, once again, he resumed his ascent. That's when he heard the first clap of thunder and felt drops drumming his helmet. The storm wasn't afar off; it was on top of him! Looking up, he caught some rain in his eyes and quickly swiped the drops away, clearing his vision.

CRACK!!! Another rumble of thunder ripped right overhead. The sky grew black as midnight choking out what was left of daylight. Before he could fully grasp the severity of the moment, a bolt of lightning struck a dried pine tree just off to his right. The flames lit up like fireworks sending shards of bark and needles in all directions. The impact threw him backward, down…down…down where he'd already been. His anchor pulled away, and he lost control.

"I'm gonna die!"

Everything went black.

***

It may have been hours that he lay in the dark. The first awakenings were to the sound of "Hi-ram? Hi-ram?" Rain was splashing his face and as he struggled to get up pain shot through his back. Still, he heard a voice calling, "Hi-ram? Hi-ram?"

"I'm here! Down here!" There was no answer. Not even the wind whispered his name. There was only the steady drumming of rain on his face. He was in a shower, flat on his back in pain, with no way to turn off the spigot. So, there he lay. Nobody had climbed with him. Nobody knew where he was, exactly. How would he find help?

Even if he had been able to move it was so dark that he couldn't see to climb up or down. For the first time, he was afraid, very afraid. Where had he landed? Was it safe to move or would he fall again if he tried? He stayed put. All of these questions swam in his head like a sea of confusion. He felt like he was drowning!

"Hi'M...Hi'M..." he heard this time like someone was greeting him, but his name wasn't "M."

"Who are you? What do you want with me?"

There was no answer, only blackness and the steady falling of rain. Every once in a while, he saw flashes of light and heard thunder rolling off in the distance. When he attempted to lift his head slightly to see if he could identify his position, a flare of pain shot through his neck and threw him into unconsciousness again.

He dreamed—or was it a vision? He was at his friend's Bar Mitzpah, and a chorus of people kept raising their glasses, saying, "L'chaim! To life!" It sounded a lot like his name, "L'Hiram!" He didn't understand. He wasn't Jewish, and it was his friend's party, not his. Why would they be calling his name? He fell into a deep sleep overcome by such strangeness.

At first light, Hiram's eyes opened to red sky. The rain was no longer hitting him in the face. He was wet and cold. He tried to rise again but felt nothing—no pain, no movement. Bile rose in his throat, and he began to panic.

"Help me! Help me! Somebody help me!" he cried out.

It seemed as though he had cried out for hours and hours with no answer. At least his voice still worked! Then, all at once, he heard a voice like a soft whisper on the wind. Was his mind playing games?

"I AM..."

The voice he heard this time seemed to calm him. He was no longer afraid. He no longer felt alone. He just lay there under the open sky and waited patiently. Then he thought he heard the clanging of a bell. His mind was really playing tricks on him—or was it? There was a disturbance above his head. Rocks and gravel sprinkled toward his face so he closed his eyes in response. He kept them closed for some time until he no longer felt debris hitting him in the face. "Pah-tooey!" He spat out the grit that had gathered around his mouth. When he opened his eyes, he saw the snout of a pink bighorn sheep. It snorted in his face. He jumped! The sheep jerked back in surprise.

"Baa!" the sheep bleated.

"Next, I'll be seeing pink unicorns!" Hiram had to laugh. Could any of this be real? Seriously?

"HIRAM? Are you Hiram?" he heard a voice say. It sounded like the voice of God, but he really wasn't religious by any stretch of the imagination. He did love all of creation, but the voice filled him with wonder.

Hiram could only answer weakly, "I'm Hiram! Here I am! Who wants to know? Are you God?"

Laughter lit up the ranger's whole body as his head peeked from behind a boulder. His eyes fell on Hiram.

"I've been called a lot of things…but God was never one of them. I'm Ranger Rick from Rocky Mountain Rescue. Your parents enacted a search when you didn't come home last night. I'm here to help you. Don't move! I'll get the team to help." With that, he got on his walkie-talkie and gave his position to the team. They would bring a stretcher.

COLLECTIONS OF THE HEART

"Hold on, Hiram, help is on the way. It's lucky you landed where you did."

"Why's that?"

"You landed in an aerie."

"What's that?"

"An eagle's nest! Without it, you would have fallen a good 300 feet down on top of boulders, and we wouldn't be having this conversation."

"I saw a pink sheep before. What's with that?"

"That's Ram-a-Sees, part of my high mountain rescue team. He's pretty good at finding wayward climbers, huh? As for the pink part, he's not. It appears you have blood in your eyes from the fall, and it's coloring your vision."

"Oh..." was all he could think to say. Only a few moments later they heard the welcoming sound of a whirlybird overhead. The helicopter created quite a draft and Hiram again closed his eyes to avoid any debris that might blow. A stretcher was let down on some cables like a spider dropping from the ceiling, but it was not within the rescuers' reach. They decided to fly up to a flat spot up the mountain and rappel down to Hiram. It would be a tricky rescue with danger all its own. Hiram opened his eyes again and waited for what seemed like half an hour. Soon two orange vested men appeared in harnesses with ropes and the stretcher. They were swift in rappelling to where he was stranded, and they did a bit of deft climbing to the edge of the aerie. The thing about eagles' nests is that they are built on the edge of nowhere to keep their precious offspring from predators. The same protection for the birds was proving a hazard in this case. Hiram was nearly unreachable.

One emergency team member had a backboard and neck collar. Hiram's head would be strapped to keep his neck stable for transport. Hiram wondered, *how did these guys know how to make such difficult movements and still carry someone else out?* He was in awe as they worked skillfully. By now, he felt no pain anywhere on his body, and while he was glad at that, he was also a little bit concerned—arms, hands, feet…not even a tingle of feeling.

Once the stretcher was lifted above the top ridge Ranger Rick and Ram-a-Sees scaled the face to where the helicopter waited. He gave the thumbs-up signal to the pilot, and Hiram was whisked off to the area hospital best suited to spinal traumas. He whispered a prayer of thanks, along with a special request for healing. By all outward signs, Hiram was going to have a long road to recovery.

***

COLLECTIONS OF THE HEART

Ma and Pa were waiting at the Denver hospital ahead of the copter. They were thankful Hiram had been found and rescued, but that ugly gnawing in Ma's stomach was now in Pa's, too. This was serious.

The clock in the waiting room seemed tediously slow. They paced, drank bad coffee, and paced some more. It had been two hours since their son had been brought in, and they still needed to hear something other than, "He's alive. The trauma team is still assessing his condition. We'll give you an update just as soon as we have something to report."

Finally, Pa had had enough. "I don't care what they say…I'm going IN…" Just then, the double doors from the emergency trauma center opened out and a doctor came to brief them.

"Are you Hiram's parents?"

"Yes!" they affirmed in unison.

"He's one lucky boy to be alive…he's stabilized now, but he'll have a long road to fully recover. He's broken his back in two places and also one vertebra in his neck." He gestured with the chart, "Why don't we step down the hall into my office to review the x-rays. We can discuss treatment more privately there."

Ma gulped down the lump that was in her throat. "May we see him?" She pleaded through teary eyes.

COLLECTIONS OF THE HEART

"Yes, walk with me and don't be alarmed at the headgear. It's there to keep his neck stable." The scene that awaited them was a bit overwhelming. It was a scene out of a horror movie. Hiram didn't look at all like himself. His face was swollen and mostly black with bruising. Monitors and tubes, dials, and dripping bags were hooked up to different body parts. The headgear looked like a giant vise clamped around him like a dinosaur swallowing its prey. Ma wanted to smother him with kisses and hugs, but there was no clear path to his face. For now, she could only blow kisses. The bed was equipped with a mirror so that Hiram could see her while he remained perfectly flat on his back. A tear slid down his cheek.

"Ma, I'm so sorry to mess things up like this on my birthday!"

"Oh, Hiram, with all the excitement, I never got to bake your cake. We'll celebrate when you're feeling up to it, okay?"

***

Six weeks and three surgeries later, Hiram still had no feeling in his legs. His arms and hands worked again, which was good. Soon he could begin Physical Therapy (PT) and re-teach his legs how to walk. His new home would be a convalescent facility for the foreseeable future. Oh, how he longed for his mountain and to be able to climb again! The strong muscles that he had built-up through climbing were now flaccid and weak. He thought how true the saying was, "If you don't use it you lose it."

Each day Ma would bring his schoolwork, which they fit in between his PT sessions. It was even hard to grasp a pen or pencil. It would be a long, hard climb to get back to where he once was. Before long, he treated PT like mountain climbing training between parallel bars and caught up. By afternoon he was usually exhausted and took a nap until dinner. Oh, how he missed his mom's cooking! Once a week on Saturdays, a local youth group visited, sang a few songs, and told Bible stories about the heroes of faith. It was all new to him, and he eagerly navigated the hallways to the dining hall in his wheelchair to attend. From each story, he drew strength: *Daniel in the Lion's Den* taught him to trust that everything would work out for good; Samson's strength inspired him to work his muscles, and the story of Moses made him wonder about his own encounter on the mountain and hearing the strange whispers on the wind. Was God trying to get his attention? He would often think on these things once he was back in his room alone. He didn't even know how to go about contacting God, but he was starting to believe that his rescue had been something of a miracle beyond the abilities of mere mortal men.

"God, if you're there…it's me, Hiram. Thanks for the rescue!" He felt peace surround him and thought he heard a very quiet whisper like the wind on the mountain.

COLLECTIONS OF THE HEART

"I AM."

***

Six months later, as the spring snows melted on the parking lot, Hiram walked out of the convalescent facility on crutches but under his own power. By medical standards, considering the severity of his trauma, he was a walking miracle. All of his body parts were working again. It was almost as though nothing had happened, yet something had very definitely happened. He had been broken, and now he was whole. He had been lost, and now he was found. He was unaware of God, and now he had a deep, abiding, first-hand relationship with the One Who made the mountains he so loved to climb. He had an uncommon strength, much like Samson. The time he'd spent in rehabilitation had been a blessing in disguise, a college course in courage and overcoming hardships. He'd had a lot of time to consider his future. He would be graduating soon and had formed a thought about what to pursue next. He couldn't wait to be home with his parents and discuss it around a home-cooked meal. His father helped him into the truck, tossed the crutches in the rear, and asked, "Hiram, are you ready to start climbing again?"

"Almost, dad. Maybe not today, but soon…"

They both smiled as Dad started the engine and backed out of the parking space to take the long road home. Today, he would give anything to see his son once again climb the rock face behind their home.

***

It was still a bit of a challenge to climb the steps onto the porch on crutches, but he managed without falling backward. Dad unlatched the front door, and Hiram gave it a shove with one of the crutches.

"Surprise! SURPRISE! Surprise!" There were shouts from a room full of faces amid floating balloons and a colorful banner reading, "Welcome home, King of the Mountain!" He couldn't quite take it all in. His mother smothered him with kisses, and friends came forward to shake his hand or clap him on the back. He looked in puzzlement at his mom, "What's all this?"

"Well, it seems SOMEone skipped out on his seventeenth birthday! After nearly eight months, don't you think it's about high time we celebrate?"

"Awesome! So, where's the cake? I'm starving!"

Everybody laughed. There was so much more than cake—all of Hiram's favorite foods were on the long buffet table: fried chicken, homemade biscuits, Mom's pink Jell-O salad with marshmallows in it, baked beans, and everything was served with a big heap of love. He could hardly take it all in. The kids from the youth group hall all come along with Ranger Rick, though he didn't bring Ram-A-Sees. After the feeding frenzy, everyone settled into comfortable conversation as Mom started bringing presents for him to open. The youth group gave him his own Bible inscribed with his name in gold letters along with a storybook of his favorite biblical heroes. His parents resupplied him with some new climbing ropes, anchors, and other gear. Ranger Rick's present was a box of flares. "Just in case there's a NEXT time you need rescuing." Even Ram-A-Sees had sent a gift, a cowbell like the one that had been on his collar while on mountain rescue duty.

"Thanks, everyone! I'm so thankful for you all. I probably wouldn't be celebrating today if even one of you wasn't in my life. So much for the mushy stuff…"

One of the kids grabbed his guitar and began a hearty round of:

> My God is so big, so strong, and so mighty
>
> There's nothing my God cannot do
>
> He made the mountains, and He made the valleys
>
> The stars are His handiworks, too (CLAP, CLAP)
>
> My God is so big, so strong, and so mighty
>
> There's nothing my God cannot do
>
> For you and you

COLLECTIONS OF THE HEART

And you and you and you!

They all pointed to one another and laughed late into the evening. It had been a wonderful homecoming.

***

After a few more days of PT, Hiram felt strong enough to abandon the crutches and test his climbing skills scaling only the lower set of boulders behind the cabin. He soon discovered that the muscles you use in therapy are not quite the same as the ones you use in climbing. His first few attempts were not very fruitful. He tired quickly and worked up a good sweat. Mom was all too happy to feed him each day. She had missed cooking for her son and was so grateful to have him close enough to hug again.

One night after a wonderful dinner of hearty beef stew and cornbread, Hiram cleared his throat and announced to his parents, "I think that after graduation I would like to work for the forestry department, particularly in the mountain rescue unit."

His mom and dad exchanged glances and wiped their mouths on their napkins. It was his father who first said, "Son, you know there are many years of training ahead of you, college classes, medical training, and so on?"

"Yes, I'm aware of that. I already spoke with Ranger Rick. I learned something up there on that mountain, Dad, even in the bad time. Sometimes you have to come upon a crisis before you decide which way to go. I think I'm ready to learn everything necessary to rescue others. It takes a TEAM, and I was acting alone. I wanted to be the best for *myself* because it fed my ego, but now I want to be part of the best team to help *others*."

His mom broke into the conversation. "I think I've always known since you were little, that whatever you became in life would include climbing. I'm not really surprised. You have a gift, son. It's time you put it to good use."

"Mom, can we raise some bighorn sheep to train for the good of mankind?"

"You always have to push the limits, don't you?" She laughed, but in her heart, she knew she had already answered *yes*.

***

EPILOGUE

It had been a long climb up the 10,000-foot front range with his team of junior rangers. After rappelling down again and gathering all the gear back into the forestry truck he put on his ranger hat, strapped on his seat belt, and took off with his trainees to log in their time back at base camp. It was now his tenth year as a bona fide Rocky Mountain Ranger. He chatted with his passengers about their experience. Most of them were as eager as he had been

COLLECTIONS OF THE HEART

back in elementary school. They drove past a playground, and he slowed the truck down and pointed.

"There's one!"

"One *what*?"

"A future rescue ranger, a climber."

"Where?"

"Up there, walking across the top of the monkey bars?"

"How do you know, anyway?"

"I just *KNOW*. It takes one to know one!"

THE END

"Humble yourselves in the sight of the Lord and He will lift you up."

James 4:10 KJV

COLLECTIONS OF THE HEART

IN THE COMPANY
by Cindy Tesar

He exited the overwhelmingly noisy corporate offices, hunched under the weight of his pending decision, toting only a briefcase and a heavy heart. Stopping briefly at a vendor, he purchased a long sleeve of freshly popped corn and darted across the traffic circle between cars to the little park. Securing his favorite flattened spot beneath the weeping willow, he laid out the picnic meticulously as he had done every day in his life. Carefully slipping off his Manolo Blahniks, he spread out the red tartan plaid blanket from within the briefcase. Using the lid's surface for a table, he carefully set out his tuna salad sandwich on whole wheat with extra mayo, just the way he liked it. He presented the vintage bottle of Pellegrino Water for approval, laid it to the side of the long sleeve of popcorn, and waited. As if in silent prayer, he leaned his head back against the crying tree, heaving a sigh, and closed his eyes. Willow blossoms tickled his nose, and he soon heard the skittering of a bushy gray squirrel descending the trunk above his head. His lunch date had arrived, and she loved popcorn. They dined, he smiled, and then she fled without a good-bye; pouches full. Sensing someone by his side, he looked but so no one. Again, he smiled and felt a gentle caress of sorts.

COLLECTIONS OF THE HEART

Savoring each bite of his sandwich and the occasional crunch of celery, he tore off little bits near the crust and tossed them on the banks of the pond. Soon, he lured mama blue-winged teal and her brood to the beachhead. There they pecked and tore at the feast. Dragging the last vestiges with them into the green water, mama swam ahead with eight fuzz balls in tow like a toy drawn with invisible strings. The man, totally heartened with his encounter, stood to his feet. An unsolicited laugh erupted from somewhere deep inside. Again, he felt embraced by an unseen force.

 The freshly mown grass was cool on his bare feet and released its fragrance as he padded along the brink, observing the antics of water bugs skating on the surface and the occasional peek-a-boo of frogs from beneath the floating lotus. Filled now, to the most delightful capacity, he returned to pack-up the valise. Shaking crumbs from the blanket, he carefully folded it and tucked the memories in with each crease. He slipped on his stockings and shoes without lacing them and packed up everything but the popcorn and his water, the last of which he drained. In a grand gesture, he flung the popped kernels into the wind for the pigeons that would soon gather. He crumpled the bag and deposited it into the trash receptacle right next to the recycle bin, where he dropped his green bottle. He padded back across the traffic circle to the mania of the office building. The lobby was bustling with activity and a cacophony of electronic gadgets in service. He heaved a

COLLECTIONS OF THE HEART

sigh of relief as the lift doors opened. He stepped into the enveloping soft music that accompanied his ride to the top floor, where the elevator stopped and *dinged* his arrival. He walked the long hallway to the corner office with the ebony desk overlooking his vast empire. Quickly tapping a note on his computer and sending it to print, he bent over and tied his shoes for the journey. He retrieved the note, signed and precisely positioned it atop the desk, picked up his briefcase, and rode the elevator back down to street level. As he crossed the lobby, he smiled and acknowledged those who had attended him through the years; janitors, valets, concierge`, security, and the doormen. They noted a transformation from his normally gruff and preoccupied demeanor, a new light in his countenance.

Pushing through the revolving door, he had a mental image of the words, "I quit!" inked from his computer. It made him beam broadly. Exiting to the sidewalk, he offered his arm to an unseen entity, and she took it as he strode away from the seventh of a six-figure income, this time in pursuit of the true riches. Joy was now his constant companion. She took the offered arm, and as he glanced over his shoulder, caught a glimpse of Goodness and Mercy following closely behind.

Psalm 23:6 "Surely goodness and mercy shall follow me all the days of my life, and I will dwell in the house of the LORD forever."

COLLECTIONS OF THE HEART

IT IS YOUR CHOICE
by Jim Hutcheson

While on the practice green at our local golf course, two maintenance men came by in their cart. They slowed down when God directed me to talk to them. I don't know how our conversation started, however, in a few moments, I told them that they were at a fork on the road of life. It is your choice; you can go the world's way or God's way.

If you choose the world's way, you will always seek and never find the life you want. Oh, you will find happiness, contentment, purpose, joy, and dedication for a moment, but they will all be fleeting and never lasting. You will never have lasting fulfillment or contentment.

If you choose God's way, He will give you dedication, purpose, happiness, contentment, fulfillment, and joy. You will lose nothing but gain everything by choosing Christ or God's way. When you die, your soul continues to live forever in Heaven if you choose Christ.

If you choose the world's way, your soul will live in hell forever. Hell is a place of torment or a place where your soul will burn forever.

Let's say you live 100 years and on the road of life, that equals 1 inch. The peak of Mount San Gorgonio is about 30 miles from here. If you take 30 X 5280 X 12 X 100=15,838,800 years down the road of life. In this length of time, you are just barely getting started down that road.

If you use the distance from here to New York City X 5280 X 12

X 100 = # of years, you still are not there. You will never get to the end of eternity because it has no end.

COLLECTIONS OF THE HEART

Where do you want to spend eternity, in Heaven or Hell, happiness or torment? It is your choice.

As for me, I enjoy serving Christ here, and I will spend eternity in Heaven.

The older man then told me that his mother, a pastor, talked to him along the same lines, but it sounds a lot different from me.

COLLECTIONS OF THE HEART

JAWING
by Jim Hutcheson

From the annals of the Wild West is a story from my cattle ranch on the Red River in the Oklahoma Territory.

I was sitting on my veranda on a very hot late summer day when I heard a commotion out at the hitching rail. Mossing out, there was "Running Bear," a Black Foot Brave, and "Joaquin Garcia," a wanted Mexican from Mexico jawing at each other fiercely. As I approached them, I said, "What are you boys jawing about?"

Joaquin replied, "This dumb Injun thinks he is a better shot than I am, and everybody in the territory knows I am the best."

Running Bear, slipping his hand into his pocket, said, "That ain't so, I can outshoot this d** Mexican any day of the week." Throwing a silver dollar way up in the air, drawing his 44 Frontier six, and firing one round, the dollar landed right in front of his feet with a hole right in the center. Picking it up, he said, "You can't outshoot this."

Joaquin said, "Throw it way up this time," and running; Bear threw it. Joaquin aiming his old 30-0-6 sharps rifle fired one round, and the silver dollar landed right at Running Bear's feet again. Picking it up, "Ah, you missed."

Joaquin, "No, I didn't. Everybody knows a 44 leaves a bigger hole than an 0-6. I went right through your hole."

After some more jawing, they headed off together downriver to the "Rattle Snake Saloon" in the little town of Red River.

Now, the bigger question is, which one is the bigger liar? Had Running Bear's round hit the silver dollar it would not have landed close to us due to the force of the round hitting the dollar. Had Joaquin's round gone through the hole already in the dollar, the force would have still carried it out around ten feet or more from where we were standing. The hole had to be in the dollar before it was thrown.

This was life in the Wild West.

Law West Of The Pecos
by Jim Hutcheson

Capt., Snake, and I decided to go out west after the war. There was nothing left for us in Georgia. Paw was killed at the Battle of Fredericksburg by one of them Damn Yankee artillery shells. Maw and the young' uns were killed when Gen. Sherman's troops burned our plantation--house, barns, drying rooms, and crops. Whatever was left the bank or them Dam-Yankee Carpetbaggers will get. Our plantation was along the Oconee River, south of Atlanta.

Capt. wasn't really a Capt. in the Army; he was a Corporal, but he liked to be called Capt. so we humor him.

Now, Snake was a half-breed. His paw was a Seminole Indian, and his maw was a plantation owner. Snake could move through the brush quieter than a copperhead in dry leaves. He had a real mean temper, so you never wanted to cross him.

We were at the battle of Vicksburg when one of them Dam-Yankee snipers fired at Snake and hit his mess kit, just before supper. It ruined his supper, and he was mad. That night along about 9:30 he took off his boots and put on his moccasins and slipped through our picket lines over to theirs's. He came up behind one of their pickets and slit his throat but he didn't have a mess kit, so he went after the next one. This time he took his Bowie knife and cut him from his belly to his chest gutting him. He took his mess kit and came back through our lines. It had US stamped into it, but Snake couldn't read so it didn't matter. He just washed off his knife and went to sleep just as if it was all in a day's work.

When the war was over we planned on going to the goldfields of California, but when we came across a ranch in Southern New Mexico that needed some hands, we decided to stay. We've been punching cattle for over two years on this spread. It's over 1500 acres and out in the flats of Southern New Mexico.

Late Friday afternoon, as we came in from the range, Mr. Baldwin, owner of the
"Flying W" ranch met us and said, "Boy's, you've been

COLLECTIONS OF THE HEART

working real hard out on the range. Take a couple days off and go into town and wet your whistle." He then handed us each $50.

El Paso is south of us, and Las Cruces is northwest. El Paso is larger and about 3 miles farther than Las Cruces. Rosas's Cantina is in El Paso and has lots of rotgut tequila. The Mesquite Saloon is in Las Cruces has some of the smoothest whiskey you ever tasted. They say that old Tom takes a couple of wagons down to New Orleans 2 or 3 times a year and brings back barrels of good southern whiskey.

The next morning we rode to Las Cruces, tied up our horses at the hitching post, and went in for a drink. As we walked through the swinging doors, we noticed 3 Dam-Yankee Carpetbaggers sitting at a table playing poker, two drifters listening to every word old Curley was saying, and several other regular cowhands.

Everybody called him Curley, but he is as bald as a queue ball, 5'2", and is an old prospector. When he comes into the bar, he hands Tom, the bartender, a few nuggets or some gold dust, which Tom weighs and then gives him that much whiskey. Those drifters were hanging on to every word he said. He talks a lot when he has had a few shots of whiskey.

COLLECTIONS OF THE HEART

No one knows for sure if he has a couple of mines up in the San Andres Mountains or if he found the gold that Geronimo buried there. A few years back, there was a wagon load of gold coming from the goldfields escorted by 20 Blue Coats. Geronimo ambushed and killed all of them, took the gold and headed for the mountains, and hid it. There was a detachment of Blue Coats coming from the East, and when they heard about it they hunted high and low but never did find the gold or the Apaches. Some of Curley's dust sure looks like it was scraped off a bar instead of coming from a mine.

Curley's old mule out at the hitching post was beginning to bay, so he finished his drink and headed for his mine. Those drifters talked real low like they were planning something, and then they left. We figured that they were going to follow and jump him, but we knew he was a sly old fox and knew they were coming. He led them on a path that went right under a large outcropping of rocks. When he had passed the rocks, he slapped his mule on its flank, and it took off for home. He scurried up the rocks to where he had a couple of kegs of black powder hid, and when them drifters were in the right place, he lit the fuse. They are now under about 2 ton of rock.

COLLECTIONS OF THE HEART

At the Mesquite Saloon, those poker players were just playing for fun, waiting for some cowpoke to come through the door so they could take his money. Billy came in, saw them, and asked, "Is this a closed game, or can anyone sit in?" The card shark said, "Sure, Your money is as good as the next man's."

People around here just called him "Billy," but some called him "Billy the Kid," and others called him, well we won't get into that. There is nothing Billy likes better than a good clean game of poker.

After about 4 or 5 hands, Billy was up about $20, and the gambler was dealing. Everyone had anti-upped, and the other two guys folded. Now it was just Billy and the gambler. The gambler said, "I raise you five," and threw a $5 gold piece into the pot. Billy took a hard look at his cards and threw $5 into the pot and said, "I call." The gambler laid his cards down---Ace of Hearts, Ace of Diamonds, Ace of Spades, a 2 of Hearts, and a 6 of Clubs, and he reached for the pot. Billy says's "Hold on there," as his right-hand slips off the table. He draws his 44 Colt and fires right through the table, hitting the gambler in the chest and knocking him and his chair over backward. A lot of blood spattered all over the floor.

COLLECTIONS OF THE HEART

One of his companions started to reach for the derringer in his coat, but Billy swinging his 44 around, said, "If you want to join him, keep reaching." Now both of the carpetbaggers held their hands away from their sides and just kind of shuffled backward.

Sheriff Hawkins had heard the shot and was now coming through the swinging doors.... seeing what happened says, "Billy, why did you shoot him?" Billy answers, "Because he was cheating, and you know I can't stand people who cheat at cards. Just look at his hand." As the sheriff looks, Billy turns his hand over and says, "There ain't two aces of spades in a deck, and I was dealt this one."

Looking over at his companions, Sheriff Hawkins says, "Boy's, there is a couple of shovels out n' back, follow the path and dig a hole for him. If you want to say a few words over him, that's ok." Turning and looking around the room, he say's "Juan, Slim, carry this dam cheater out of here up to boot hill."

Awhile later, them Damn Yankee Carpetbaggers came back dusting the dirt off their coats, and Sheriff Hawkins says, "If you boys have horses, be out of town before sundown. If not, there is a stage about sun up headed for Yuma or another one headed for Santa Fe about 10 o'clock. If yer still here at noon, I am going to lock you up. Judge Roy Bean will be through here in 3 or 4 weeks on his circuit. Now I am a telling ya, he won't like the likes of you. Here bouts, he is known as the hanging judge. Enough said."

And That Was Law West Of the Pecos

PHANTASMAGORIA
by Dennis Knotts

Michael Jensen stepped into the hallway. It was an empty hallway with only the door he had passed through visible. But he had been in empty hallways before. It was all about plausible deniability. He stepped to the far wall and recited:

"Jensen, Michael, Lieutenant! United Federation Force. Serial number EDJ 093-567-11098/34518. Reporting to QR 37."

"Welcome to QR 37, Lieutenant Jensen." The wall slid back, and an older man in a lab smock stepped forward and extended his right hand. "I'm Dr. Keebler."

As Lieutenant Jensen took Dr. Keebler's offered hand, there was a pinprick in his palm. Before the pinprick registered, everything went black, and he began to fall.

Jensen shook his head, trying to get his eyes to clear. "How long was I out?"

"That information will remain classified. Our location, as well as our work, is not public (nor military) knowledge. It would be safe to say that you were nowhere near the hallway you entered. Are you feeling any discomfort?"

"No. It's just a habit I developed. I never like losing control of myself. It's a subconscious need to know how long everything is shut down."

"This experiment may push your sense of self-control. I assume you have been briefed."

"You are attempting to create a space warp by bending the fabric of the space continuum, making travel of thousands of light-years possible instantaneous."

"Yes, you could travel to another galaxy with no more effort than it requires to take a step. We could do away with most of the space fleet."

"General Briggs said your probes came back scrambled," Jensen suggested.

"Not the probes, but the images."

"So, no one knows what happens." Jensen probed.

"I take it that General Briggs mentioned the test subjects?"

"Yes," Jensen said no more than that. He would let Keebler decide how much information he should know.

"We've had no fatalities," Dr. Keebler offered. Jensen continued to look him in the eyes. "We are not sure what happened. The animals were in a state of shock. It was as if their systems were subjected to extreme emotional trauma. This is why we tried the probes, but that could not answer the question. That is why we needed a human."

"So you hope that my mind will be strong enough to not only survive the trauma but also to explain what the animals went through. Then you can determine if this program will work."

"It works. We can transport units and non-living material all over the United Federation Territory. We have both a sending and receiving unit stationed at the furthest outpost. Once we fix this problem, then we can transport you or another subject to the outpost."

"But for now…?" Jensen inquired.

"For now, we are testing the process, not the distance. We have set up a sending and receiving unit side-by-side. It will be a quick jump from the sending unit to the receiving unit right next to it. No more than six feet."

COLLECTIONS OF THE HEART

"And if I come back in shock?"

"We're hoping the human mind can deal with the unknown. If you are ready for the worse, then you should have little trouble."

"But if I come back in a state of deep shock?"

"Then we will revive you. It made no sense to work on our animals. They couldn't explain anything to us even if they became normal."

"I'd feel a little more comfortable about this if someone had tried. It'd be nice to know the shock can be overcome."

"Oh, we can use drugs and bring them out of it for short periods, but there is no way we can provide extensive therapy to make it a permanent cure."

"I can see why they did not argue about my request for hazardous duty pay." Jensen offered with a short laugh. Dr. Keebler just stared at him. The man had no concept of humor. "When am I scheduled to go?"

"We've set up a training program for you. It is to condition you to shocks and trauma. The program should last about two months, and then you go."

***

COLLECTIONS OF THE HEART

Michael moved, and there was a grace to his movements that seemed to defy the bulk of his protective suit. Over the last two months, he had been exposed to every kind of shock the scientists here could devise. There were sudden noises, deafness, sensory deprivation, blinding lights, darkness, free-fall, intense gravity, and the list went on. There had even been the occasional prank of someone dressed like an alien or monster. He worked the controls before him. Several electrical shocks tore through his fingers. He noted the pain but continued working.

Blinding lights went off in his eyes, but he worked the program without vision. Sudden noises went off. He never flinched. The floor collapsed beneath him. As he fell, he continued working the panel strapped before him. After several more surprises, the red light flashed, signaling the end of the testing. The airlock to the testing chamber opened, and Dr.

Keebler was there to greet him,

"Well done, Michael. You've passed with flying colors. We should be able to send you in another week or so."

"Why wait?"

"We need to let your mind rest. You're in peak condition, but a few of us feel a few days of rest will give you an added cushion against any trauma we might have missed."

***

Michael studied the smooth steel plates staring back at him - magnetic generators needed to create the field. A similar room was next door. Michael could feel the pressure on the metal of his suit as the fields were engaged. There was the sensation of pushing and pulling from all directions. It became a pulsing feeling. He felt as if he were fading in and out. The walls before him created the optical illusion of becoming concaved and then convexed.

The transformations made the plates appear to have come alive and were now breathing. He put his mind through his disciplines to demand perfect control. He operated the control of his suit as the needed distraction. He reached forward only to discover his fingers passed through the glove of the pressure suit. Something was wrong. Inanimate matter always traveled with the animate matter.

The lieutenant told himself it was a false image. He told himself it couldn't be happening. His breath came in short gasps as the first beads of sweat appeared on his forehead. The cooling system of the suit made no difference.

COLLECTIONS OF THE HEART

This had been the one thing they could not have prepared him for. In the tests, he always knew it was only a test. He knew that whatever they threw at him was part of the world he was familiar with. This was "*unreal*."

He forced his mind into the proper frame of thinking. He had to keep control. Even if this wasn't the real world, he could make the difference. It would take only seconds. Then it would be over. He would find himself in the other room and would be home.

A red light flashed. His mind relaxed. But he knew the test was not over. The scientists had inadvertently programmed him to respond with the flashing red light. He fought to maintain control. He needed to stay focused.

The room exploded. He saw faces exploding in slow motion. Their screams were the screams of the damned. It then dawned upon him that these were the faces of friends who were dead.

He wondered if they had opened the gates of Hell by mistake. Instantly faces of demons and ghouls appeared. They clawed at him, and his suit tore. The life-giving air hissed out in a hideous gasp. His lungs felt like they were collapsing.

COLLECTIONS OF THE HEART

The bitter cold of space began to crystallize the tissue of his throat and lungs. They were becoming brittle, and he could feel them starting to shatter.

He fought his way back into control. He told himself it couldn't be happening. He struggled to take in a breath. Every sense he had told him his lungs would splinter if he tried to breathe. He pushed his thoughts into a logical framework.

"I can still think. I'm still alive. My lungs are still getting air to my body. Breathe. BREATHE!!"

With his greatest effort, he drew in air. His lungs began to splinter. There came the intense pain of his entire chest cavity being ripped to shreds by the icy shards. Still, he inhaled. The pain stopped. It was the silence of the grave. The suit was intact.

"I'm still in control," he told himself. The faces rushed at him. "I'm in control," he assured himself. His hands began to tremble. His body began to shake violently. And then, the demons returned…and multiplied. There were thousands of them, millions.

"I'M IN CONTROL!!" he shouted, but one of the demons made a slight gesture and silence filled his ears. Then Michael's arm slammed against his faceplate. He struck his faceplate again. He tried to grab his arm to make it stop, but the other hand began to beat at the faceplate. Then there was the sound that sent waves of terror into his mind. It was the sound of glass beginning to crack – a high note ringing in his ears. A hairline fissure spread across the faceplate, and still, his hands slapped the view screen.

"They've taken over my body. They're killing me with myself. What happened to my control? When is the experiment over?" he screamed in his mind. He was sure the words were verbal but he could not hear them. In its place, a voice snarled and sent ice shooting through his veins.

"There is no escape," it rasped with a guttural sound from vocal cords long unused to speech. "You have entered our domain. You are ours. You have broken more than the space continuum. You are in the spirit realm. We can keep you here for as long as we wish. Time has no meaning in this world. You are OURS!"

The figures swarmed over him like a crashing wave. He lost control. He was battered down. He could no longer remember how long it had been. From the pit of his soul, he screamed. It was the scream of a lost soul flung into the depths of Hell. The analogy struck him. Michael remembered a discussion from his past – back to his days of innocence. His grandmother had said something to him when he had

COLLECTIONS OF THE HEART

awakened from a nightmare as a thunderstorm crashed overhead. What had she said? He had to remember. But the battering continued. His mind was a jumble. He could barely think. Then the instruction from his grandmother flashed before him. He grabbed it the way a drowning man grabs a floating straw in the churning sea.

"HELP ME, JESUS!!!"

At that exact instant, something caught his hand and tore him loose from the terrifying horde. Whatever had hold of him was enough to frighten even the demons. As his plea died on his lips, he saw the room returning around him. He collapsed. His suit was in shreds. They would never be able to explain what had happened. He knew there would be long months, maybe years, of treatment ahead of him. He wasn't sure what he should say. To speak the truth would condemn him to an institution. To keep quiet would send another poor soul to his doom. He would have to find something to say. Some way to halt the project.

He studied his hand. This was the same hand he had stretched out for help. His mind played the scene before him over and over. He could think of no other way to describe the hand that held him and pulled him free than the one description which had been used for centuries. The hand that freed him had been...nail-scared.

COLLECTIONS OF THE HEART

© Copyright 1983, Dennis Knotts

Reprinted from *THE GIFT OF THE UNICORN.*

All rights reserved, used with permission.

RESCUED BY AN ANGEL
by Jim Hutcheson

September 26th was a rather hot day in Southern California. I drove to Big Bear and then to Holcomb Valley, which is in the San Bernardino Mountains near Big Bear, for the weekend to celebrate my birthday. I was in Holcomb Valley many years ago but never to the east end.

Holcomb Valley is very rich in the history of San Bernardino County. The largest gold strike south of the mother lode was made here when the mother lode began to play out. Its heyday was from 1860 to 1880. During that time, 2,000 miners in the area almost merited the San Bernardino County seat.

I was here not as a weekend prospector but to take pictures of historical sites and relics. There are still lost mines in the area and a replica of Van Dusen's log cabin. He was the local Blacksmith and the owner of a lost mine. The sites of

COLLECTIONS OF THE HEART

Belleville, named for the first baby born in Holcomb Valley, the original gold site, the hanging tree, stamp mills, etc. can still be seen. However, today there isn't a lot left at most of these sites. Holcomb Valley became famous when Billy Holcomb wounded a bear, tracked it into the valley, and while crossing a stream, noticed gold glistening in the water.

I reached Holcomb Valley via the Van Dusen Canyon Road, which starts from HWY 18 just east of Big Bear Lake. Except for a start, this 3.9-mile dirt road was very passable. It tee's into another dirt road near the original gold discovery site and Belleville. The lost Van Dusen mine is said to be in this canyon or an adjacent one but never found.

From here, I headed east past Van Dusen's cabin to the east end of the valley, a beautiful high open valley with grass rangelands as well as pines, manzanita, and mesquite. Several miles down the road, I came to a crossroads. There was a sign at about eye level saying, "To highway 18", and down at ground level another sign saying, "4 Wheel Drive and Off-Road Bikes only," which I did not notice, and I was driving my Buick. From here, it is 2.9 miles to Highway 18 via Jacoby Canyon.

At first, the road did not seem too bad but not used a lot. It was about 11:00 AM when I started down this road. The farther I went, the worse the road became. At about the 2-2.5

COLLECTIONS OF THE HEART

mile point, I came into an area of beautiful rose quartz, and this is where my trouble began. There was a big rock in the road and on the far side of it a drop-off. My car went over the rock, and when the wheel dropped, I got hung up on its frame. My Buick is a front-wheel-drive car, and now my right front wheel is just spinning in the air. I tried putting rocks and brush under the wheel to get traction, but this did not work. In this steep canyon, my cell phone did not work, so there was no way to call for help.

About 2 PM, two guys on off-road bikes came by. They couldn't help me but said that they would notify the sheriff that I needed help as soon as they arrived where they were going. By the time they got to the Bar and ordered a few drinks, they forgot about me.

Around 3 PM, the shadows in the canyon grew long. I decided that I would have to spend the night here and walk out in the morning. Walking with my cane over slippery quartz in the dark, even with my flashlight, "*no, thank you.*"

While driving down the canyon, I had noticed a lot of wildlife but nothing to be concerned about. However, there are a few bears and big cats in some remote areas of these mountains. My biggest concern was meeting up with Sasquatch. They have been seen in these mountains in the not too distant past.

COLLECTIONS OF THE HEART

There have been bones and artifacts found of Sasquatch in 48 of our 50 states. Nothing found in Roade Island or Hawaii. In Southern California, evidence of Sasquatch has been found on Santa Catalina Island, in the wilderness area of the San Gabriel Mountains near the Devils Punch Bowl, in the wilderness area of the San Bernardino Mountains near Big Bear, and also in the Santa Ana River Canyon, and in the wilderness area of the San Jacinto Mountains near Idyllwild.

About 4 PM, God sent me an Angel in a big off-road vehicle with a winch on the front of it. The driver and his girlfriend were camping in the West end of Holcomb Valley near Fawnskin. They decided to take the long way to Big Bear, and when they got to the crossroads saw the sign and thought, *why not try it.*

They winched me off the rock, turned around, and started back up the canyon. I now backed up, turned around, and started up the canyon. While turning to start up the canyon, I hit a sharp shard of rose quartz, which went through the sidewall of my right front tire. I am now stuck again.

When they did not see me behind them, they stopped, came back, and then drove me to a motel in Big Bear City. It was now about 8 PM, and there were several cafes near the motel, but none of them open. However, I found a place where I could buy a couple of candy bars and a bag of pretzels, enough to tide me over till breakfast. I notified the sheriff to cancel my call for help, which they knew nothing about.

The next morning I contacted "Big Bear Off-Road Recovery & Services." They picked me up, and we went to recover my car. About a mile down Jacoby Canyon, Steve, the driver, said that this is the point where last week they rescued an old prospector in his truck. Continuing down the road, Steve asked me, "How did you ever get this far down this road?" I answered, "This is the kind of road that I learned to drive on."

When we arrived at a point where we could see my car, Steve found a place where he could turn his rescue rig around and then back it closer. He was now about 100 feet from my car. From here, he winched my car onto his rig.

As we started up the canyon, Steve said, "Keep your window closed," and I soon learned why. As we passed a prominent outcrop of rose quartz, a big rattlesnake was laying there, all coiled sunning himself. Watching the snake through my side mirror, it suddenly sprang at the trailer. Its tail had not cleared my mirror when I turned and looked through Steve's mirror, and its image was moving across his mirror.

While stationed in the Air Force in Kansas, where we had a "Rattle Snake Roundup" every year, I had seen some big rattlers. However, I think this one was probably the longest.

About 50 feet farther up the canyon, Steve stopped the rig and checked that there were no snakes on the trailer. From the comments made, I assume sometime in the past, he must have brought a snake back to his shop on the trailer.

I settled up my bill, bought a used tire to replace my front blown tire, and headed home.

My angel may have been a man, but he was sent to me by God. There is no question in my mind about that. If God was trying to get my attention, He got it, and not a coincidence.

Disclaimer: Views expressed in this account belong solely to the author of the story, not necessarily of the Anthology's contributors and compiler.

COLLECTIONS OF THE HEART

SPRING TONIC
by Cindy Tesar

"You're my place of quiet retreat; I wait for your Word to renew me." (Psalm 119:114)

The way up the mountain hadn't always seemed this difficult. Her breath was coming in gasps as the old woman paused in the trek halfway up the trail that cut a rugged path through twists and switch-backs in its icy shadows. Leaning heavily over her gnarled walking stick, she inhaled the heady fragrance of pine yet damp with morning dew. God had strewn His best strands of translucent pearls upon spider webs between the trees. Butterflies and bees darted in and out of the Mexican sage and sweet brush, serenaded by scrub jays. Spring paraded just ahead. Patches of snow still skirted the northern nooks and crannies.

"What's that, you say?" She cupped her ear to catch the conversation with the swollen creek, just beginning its noisy rush over smooth stones. "Babble, babble…that's it? Well, then, babble-on, I say!"

She dug her staff into the dirt like stabbing a green bean and leaned into her upward climb. It was a ritual repeated every vernal equinox, the opening of the cabin. Actually, it was neither a cabin nor a shack, more of a glorified tool shed, but it was the quiet place of her ponderings, and it had been too long since she'd taken the time to cogitate there. The tragic thing about postponing such musings is that your innards tend to get backed-up. Every once in a while, one needs a good dose of spiritual Milk of Magnesia to set things in motion again, a good spring tonic.

  Huffing and puffing now, she reached the top of the trail where it cut to the right toward the overlook. Her heart took on an irregular rhythm as she caught sight of her special shelter. Coming here was sheer joy, like visiting a long-lost friend. The weathered exterior had braced itself against a good seventy-five winters followed by scorching days tanning itself in the summer sunshine. A tangle of long-spent vines curled around the covered porch supports in disarray like an old man's beard of wild hairs. Often, birds would choose this quiet bed and breakfast to build nests and launch the next generation. She approached with caution, tapping her stick along the way, never quite knowing who or what might be lurking inside or beneath the porch steps. One year, there had been a nest of rattlers minding their own procreative business. They were not delighted at her arrival, and the feeling had been mutual. All quiet today! *That's a relief!*

The steps let out a groan as she ascended three rickety planks that bowed over their supports like a very lazy U. At the top, she turned to face the overlook that always caught her breath away. *Oh, to be up where eagles hang-glide on the currents of unseen forces against a backdrop of endless mountain ranges!* Indeed, she was a good mile above cares!

Leaning her staff beside the jamb, the woman gave a good shove to the green door still swollen with winter moisture. She stepped into the interior, with the last deep freeze of winter captured within. *Brrrrr!* Quickly, she grabbed the old black coal hod and, leaving the door open, retreated to the trail in search of sunshine and kindling. The Franklin stove would soon have a *fire in the belly* if she had any say in the matter. The wind had done a thorough job of pruning dead branches and twigs, which made short work of her task. She grabbed two logs from the wood stack (no snakes there, either) and returned to erect and ignite the little tepee that always assured quick combustion. She struck the match, threw it into the little bonfire, replaced the screen, and hugged her jacket around her, waiting for warmth to penetrate.

COLLECTIONS OF THE HEART

The sanctuary was sparsely furnished, utilitarian—a small round table with two bow-back chairs nestled beneath the only window. A worn, painted blue jelly cupboard hugged the corner. Against the back wall, a canvas cot stretched out with a bedroll and army blanket folded on its end. Her treasured favorite, the rocker that had lulled each of her children to sleep in their infancy, was pulled up next to the stove. Here she sat for endless hours contemplating the meaning of life and praying. The cabin was warming now, and she felt the fire could do its work without her watchful eye. Turning to the cupboard, she searched for the old green, thermos jug, a tablecloth, and a quart canning jar. She spread the blue gingham over the table and held it in place with the blue jar, picked up the jug, and exited the cabin. The nearest point for water retrieval was halfway down the trail. Now that she was settled, it didn't seem like much of a journey. Of course, it was downhill. Her staff led the way. *All this up the trail, back down, and up again was for youngsters!*, Yet she pressed-on, thankful that she had learned to travel lightly through this life. It was necessary. There comes a tipping point in having possessions where, if you weren't careful, they would begin to possess you. Same for cares. This second visit had brought a fullness to her life; a jug of icy mountain spring water for the body and a fistful of wildflowers for the soul. She watered the canning jar vase

COLLECTIONS OF THE HEART

first and splayed out her bouquet like a bride waiting for her beloved. The tin cap of the jug became her drinking vessel. She had earned this liquid refreshment through honest labor and intended to enjoy every drop, replacing the cap to reserve the rest for some later. Picking up the iron poker, she nudged the hot side of the log upward and the warmth spread throughout the room. Replacing the screen, she gave a nod of approval to her morning's work and took a seat on her throne, drawing it a little closer to the fire. And there she sat, rocking gently to the rhythm of her heartbeat. Some are critical of those who rock, saying it's a useless activity, like worry. You expend a lot of effort but never get anywhere. She had to strenuously object, for it was here, in her rocking and pondering that many tangles, indeed, sorted themselves out. The secret is in rocking that fretful child until she settles against your heartbeat while whispering special dreams into her ear. And pleading for divine aid over her head; she sleeps.

This rocking chair was her Psalm 91 secret place. The gentle motion made her drowsy as she became mesmerized by the fire licking at the log. Leaning her head against the back of the chair, she closed her eyes. Her mind drifted through the pages of time when the whole family would gather here for picnics after a weekend hike.

COLLECTIONS OF THE HEART

Sometimes they had even slept here under starry skies and gentle breezes. The children, wild and small, would screech with delight as they swung high in the tire swing or became knights jousting with swords of wood hacked off of downed branches. She prayed they would always keep that spirit, not bogged down with tedious labor, mortgages, and cares of the world. Oh, that they too, would find the true treasures while dwelling in the secret place. Loving relationships, pursuing life's purpose with passion, using and developing God-given gifts—these were the true treasures. It wasn't long before the woman relaxed into a peaceful nap, erasing every line of tension from her face.

An easy breeze sent a flurry of dried leaves spinning in a dance across the floor. It was just enough to stir the napper. Rising from the cherished rocker, she stretched and removed her denim jacket now that inside and outside temperatures had equalized. She reached for the old corn broom propped in the corner behind the door and swept the debris into a little pile, which she scooped up with the dustpan and tossed into the fire. Returning the broom to its corner, the woman stepped out onto the porch to once again absorb the majestic vista and inhale a healthy portion of mountain freshness.

COLLECTIONS OF THE HEART

"Does a body good to spend a spell up here. Yes, yes, indeedy!" she said out loud.

Making her way over to the old oak tree, *the guardian of the north winds*, in the yard, and tested the durability of the rope from which the old tire hung and tipped out some water that had accumulated inside. With a wild notion, she hoisted herself up and gave the contraption a good swing. She was flying, wild and free! She even sang a chorus of *Down in the Valley*, crooned so often in her youth. Kicking out to swing higher, she continued, *"Hang yer head over, hear the wind blow..."* Her stomach thrilled at the giddiness of it all. As all the joy settled in, she safely landed and dismounted with a smile on her face. *Old girl's still got it!* How she loved her secret place.

Upon returning to the cabin, she opened the window and closed the door. It was time to get down to the real purpose for which she had come. Bending over the lower part of the cupboard, she retrieved the battered Gideon Bible, laid it on the table, and split it open to the Psalms. There she pulled up a chair and sat while daylight still poured through the window. She began at Psalm 91 and read, "He who dwells in the secret place of the Almighty..." And there she nestled tightly under the shadow of God's Almighty wing, right up next to his heart. Here she would stay drinking only

COLLECTIONS OF THE HEART

pure spring water and praying for His peace to engulf her. *Prayer changes us more than our circumstances.*

"Change my heart, O God. Show me the way…" Her prayer was open-ended, continuous for three days. She left the shed only to retrieve water and to use the outhouse. By day she dragged the rocker to the porch where time had worn grooves from past ponderings. At times she slept on the cot, kindling the fire again each night to take the chill off the room. Up here, she slept soundly as a bear in hibernation. On the morning of the fourth day, she sat on the porch steps feeling fully revived, and with that, she breathed out, "Thank You, Father. Amen!"

She folded the blanket and tablecloth, stowing them in the cupboard along with the Bible. The droopy wildflowers were tossed off the end of the porch along with the water. She wiped the canning jar and returned it to the cabinet, too. A few swigs from the jug drained it. That, too she stowed. Donning her jacket and grabbing the staff, she backed out of the door and pulled it securely behind her. *It is finished!*

Her face took on an angelic glow, and fairly she floated down the trail, secure in the knowledge that while she didn't know about tomorrow, she knew the One Who was already there to hold her hand. She envisioned herself lying in a meadow of wildflowers, lupines, and wild mustard and confessed, "I could die a happy woman…"

Down the trail, she heard the muffled sound of someone padding gently behind her. Surely enough, at a backward glance, friends appeared. Goodness and Mercy; her constant companions. She smiled and waved over her shoulder, making her way back down to the place she called home for now.

"Surely goodness and mercy shall follow me all the days of my life and I shall dwell in the house of the Lord forever."
Psalm 23:6

SUMMER OF 1945
by Jim Hutcheson

It was two weeks before the end of school when a man from the "University of Illinois" came to our fifth-grade class to recruit students for a special class at the university. This class started on the first Monday of summer vacation and ran for six weeks. Class time was from eight till noon.

World War II was not over; gas was still rationed, so vacations needed to be close to home. We had no plans for a vacation, so I signed up for the class. We met in front of Royce Hall and were escorted to the classroom. To get to our classroom, we passed through a room with a big two-way mirror. Seeing this mirror, we knew that young future teachers would be observing us learning how fifth graders thought and behaved.

Every morning, Mrs. Morgan, after taking roll, would have the pledge to the flag followed by a song. Our studies were reading history, orally or silently, and then answering written questions or writing about what we had just learned. This was followed by math, usually on the blackboard, and then some work from our science book.

On the first day, Mrs. Morgan wrote her name on the blackboard, turned, and said, "My name is Mrs. Morgan, and you will address me this way. Is that understood?" as she pointed to her name on the board. From this and the tone of her voice, we knew she was a very strict teacher.

During the third week, several of us got together and decided that these new young teachers should learn what fifth-grade boys are really like. Now we were not destructive, but we did teach them a few things.

The first incident was mild. Jackie, who was sitting in the back of the room, hollered, "Teach, I gotta go to the restroom right now." She turned and said sternly, "You will address me as Mrs. Morgan. Do you understand?" He replied, "Yeh, Teach, but if I don't go right now, you will have a puddle on the floor in a minute."

All the girls broke out in giggles, and the class was totally disrupted. Mrs. Moran decided she had better let him go. The class had not settled down by the time he returned. Finally, the class quieted down, and we returned to our studies. That was the only disruption that day.

COLLECTIONS OF THE HEART

Two days later, Vinnie and Chuck brought bean shooters to class. While Mrs. Morgan had her back to the class writing on the blackboard, they started shooting spit wads. This brought a lot of giggles from the girls. The boys had their bean shooters out of site before Mrs. Morgan could see them. She demanded, "Who shot these?" Naturally, no one had seen a thing, and no one could identify the shooters. I was reading in my history book while they shot spit wads.

Monday of the next week, we had a writing assignment, and I needed to use a dictionary. It was on the edge of my desk, and Mrs. Morgan was writing on the blackboard with her back to us. The room was hushed because everyone was writing when that big old dictionary slipped and hit the floor with a big bang. Startled, Mrs. Morgan turned to look at me, said, "Why did that dictionary hit the floor?" I said, "I don't know. It must have just slid off my desk." She didn't believe me.

The next incident involved Vinnie and Al. They both had rubber bands and paper clips, which they shot at each other. However, they missed, and Mrs. Morgan got hit right on her butt. She swung around and saw Vinnie with a rubber band still in his hand. She shouted, "Vinnie come here!" After a complete dressing down verbally and telling him what a terrible brat he was, he was told to stand in the corner looking only at the corner for the rest of the class period.

On Thursday, Mario brought a small garter snake to class. While Mrs. Morgan was grading some papers at her desk, and we were reading, it happened to get loose. One of the girls saw it and screamed. Now all the girls jumped up and stood on the seats of their desks frightened by that little snake. It could barely move on the highly polished floor.

Mrs. Morgan, deathly afraid of snakes, quickly called the office for someone to come and remove it. That snake couldn't hurt anybody. Any of us could have recaptured it and taken it outside and turned it loose, but she would have no part of that.

Finally, a custodian arrived with a dustpan and broom, scooped the snake up and put it in a wastebasket, and removed it from the room. Little snake is now gone, and today's class time is over. Mrs. Morgan called Mario up to her desk and, in a very firm tone, told him, "You are now expelled from this class. Do not come back."

For the rest of the six weeks, there were no more incidents. I hope that what we taught the future teachers will help them to understand fifth graders.

COLLECTIONS OF THE HEART

The Accident
by Stella McDowell

(An excerpt from "Leaving Tracks in the Snow")

Dad answered the phone. "Fritz McDowell?"

Dad acknowledged that yes, this was he. The voice continued. "Your wife and her three passengers have been in a car accident near Chippewa Falls. You need to come."

Pastor Lee Weiss, the pastor at that time, Dale Wagner from church, and Dad quickly arranged care for their kids before the three men piled into one car for a somber almost one-hundred-mile trip to the Chippewa Falls hospital.

Their wives—Joann Weiss, Joyce Wagner—Mae McDowell and an elderly widow, Sadie, had been returning from the district area women's meeting in Eau Claire, Wisconsin. An oncoming truck on the opposite side of the highway divider lost control and hit a car in front of him. The truck driver then crossed the highway divider and hit Mom's car which swung around and was hit again by the truck. The load of barn stanchions he was hauling shifted and rolled onto Mom's car. Like most accidents, the crunching and crashing of metal happened in a flash of time. Details would gradually be sorted out by the experts, but later it was proven that Mom was not at fault.

The four women were still in their seat belts and pinned in the car. Mom called out to each of her passengers by name and they each moaned a response. Paramedics arrived. As they worked to get the others out, she heard them talking. "If we could just get the driver out…she's in the worse shape." Though pain pulsed throughout her body, she was comforted to know that if she was identified as being hurt the most, then the others must be in better condition than she was.

Ambulances had already rushed the others to the Chippewa Falls hospital before Mom could be extracted from the tangled metal. One leg was broken, and her ribs were crushed from the pressure of the steering wheel. The impact to her face had been so severe that her nose had been crushed too.

The three men arrived at the Chippewa Falls hospital together in their one car. Dale was taken to his wife, Joyce. Her back was broken, and she would be taken to surgery. Pastor Lee was taken to another area to be told that his wife, Joann, had died though they had done everything they could. There was no family for Sadie, but the men were told that she too had died.

But where was Mom? Her injuries required the care of specialty doctors, so she was flown to one of the two Eau Claire, Wisconsin, hospitals since the Chippewa hospital had no eye, ear, and nose specialist.

With only one car between the three men, Dad waited with Lee until arrangements that needed to be done immediately were completed. Dale would stay at the Chippewa hospital with his wife. Then Dad and Lee drove to Eau Claire.

It was about 11 p.m. before the two men arrived. The nurse asked about the condition of the others. From her room Mom recognized Pastor's voice saying, "My wife and an older lady from the church did not survive. The other lady is in surgery in the Chippewa Falls hospital." Mom's heart sank. She hoped she would die before they walked into her room. How could she face Pastor Lee? She had been the driver.

Lee and Joann Weiss were like Mom and Dad's own kids, and like grandparents to the Weiss children. Those four children frequently stayed with Mom and Dad while the young pastor and his wife had ministry obligations. How could Mom face the children who no longer had a mother? How could she look into Lee's eyes? She silently cried out to the Lord, "Take me now before I have to face Lee."

COLLECTIONS OF THE HEART

In spite of his sorrow, Lee had a weak smile as he came into the room. "I'm so sorry, Lee," Mom said. "I heard what you said about Joann."

The pastor looked at Mom's face which was difficult to view. Her nose had been crushed and pushed inward. Dad could not hide his emotions. The room was heavy with sorrow, yet Lee gently touched Mom's hand and whispered, "Joann's better off. She's not suffering. She's with the Lord." This was not an "I hope so" kind of faith. They each knew from God's Word that what Lee had said was true.

"But you… and the children… with Joann gone..." Mom started to say. It was a sentence that didn't need to be finished. It was a time of faith overcoming the realities of the events of that August 26, 1972, day. Faith did not take away the pain of loss and grief. But faith that God was still in control was a comfort.

Family members got calls. Mary Ann and Gil were in Mundelein, Illinois. Janice was in college in the Twin Cities not far from Terry and me and our three children. She canceled her first date with Dave and went to Eau Claire instead. Terry and I packed up our kids in the Volkswagen van and headed to the hospital. Visiting rules prohibited the children from visiting their grandma so someone always stayed in or near the van with them while the adults took turns with Mom.

Over the next few weeks various visitors came and went. Sorrow, guilt, and pain were especially oppressive visitors during the nights, but God was also revealing His presence. Of all the rooms she could have been assigned to in the Eau Claire hospital, Mom had a room with a view. From her pillow she could see the glow of a lighted cross. To Mom it was a visible reminder of God's presence. He had not abandoned her. He who was also acquainted with sorrow and pain was there in the midst of her blackest times. No one understood like Jesus.

Another visitor shared, "With God there is no such word as 'accident'. In His eyes this was an incident in life. Though we cannot understand the whys, God knows, and He still has a good plan. Someday we will know…maybe in this life, maybe not until we reach heaven. Even this, we will see, is part of how He is working all things together for good for those who love Him and are called according to His purpose." The visitor was referring to Romans 8:28.

Sometimes in the middle of such sorrow it may seem insensitive to say such things. But these words did not originate in the thoughts of man, but with God. Visitors who shared Scriptures with Mom during those difficult days

COLLECTIONS OF THE HEART

brought words that addressed so many of the issues she was struggling with.

Waves of sorrow and self-imposed guilt hit her like breakers crashing onto a rugged shoreline. Two little words from Psalms 37— "Fret not" and "Fret not" and repeated a third time "Fret not"—came to her over and over. Those simple words became a weapon against depressive and destructive self-condemnation thoughts. God's Word, His truth, brought comfort, hope, and a growing understanding that God is still in control. Our days are in His hands to do with according to His will. Not that we can always understand, but that's where trust in God is fleshed out in day-by-day living.

Dad, the protector and provider for his family, had challenges too. Now he was the one to see that someone was available to care for 11-year-old Tim. Dad also needed to be there for Mom in Eau Claire and then later in La Crosse when she was well enough to be transferred to a hospital closer to home.

Though he had a good sense of business matters, dealing with insurance and accident related legal issues were all new to him. Insurance representatives and lawyers tried to stir up division between the families and bring the blame game into the picture. But Lee, Dad, and Dale stayed firm in

COLLECTIONS OF THE HEART

their unity as brothers in Christ and in their care and concern for one another. Each of them had to make decisions and make plans they had not prepared for.

Joann's funeral and burial were near her hometown and family. Ladies from the La Crosse church tried to fill in, caring for the children and with housekeeping. That was not a good solution. Next Lee brought in one of the older widows from the church as a full-time housekeeper/nanny. That also was not the answer the family needed.

Where was God's answer to the children's and Lee's needs? How could he, as a single father, continue the demands of shepherding a whole congregation plus juggle the responsibilities of his now very needy children? God was not ignorant of Lee's situation. He was moving the pieces together for an answer above and beyond anything Lee could imagine. However, at the time, living by faith and not by what could be seen was all Lee had.

Sadie had no resources for burial and no family. Several years before, Dad had bought twelve plots in a new cemetery in the area. They were cheaper by the dozen. He didn't know who would need the plots when he made the purchase, but the first plot would be for her.

Sadie had been alone for a long time until years ago, my parents invited her for Sunday dinners or just to spend a day with us often. They did this for widows in our church but since Sadie had no family, she made it clear that we belonged to her. Sadie would have been pleased to know that in death, she would be laid to rest in the family plot of those who had become like family to her in life.

Joyce had her back fused but had a long and painful hospitalization and recovery. She and Dale also had young children who needed care which she could not give for a long time. Relatives and the church family helped to fill in the empty place at home, but no one could really be an adequate substitute for a wife or mom.

God stirred hearts even of strangers to make a difference without knowing the impact of their efforts. Someplace in the mail delivery system, someone had a mystery to solve. There was a letter in a child's handwriting with a return address of only "Tim McDowell, LaCrosse, Wisconsin" and addressed simply to: Mom, The Hospital, Eau Claire, Wisconsin. They had no McDowell listed in the hospital the envelope was sent to. Someone made some calls and found that a Mrs. McDowell was in another hospital in Eau Claire. So the letter was sent there and delivered to Mom.

COLLECTIONS OF THE HEART

Totally unknown to anyone, Tim had written a note to his mom telling her about his first day of school, and about the papers sent home that needed a parent's signature. Then he wrote, "I'm giving you my $5 bill that I got for my birthday and it's not counterfeit. Please write and please get better quick. We are all praying for you. Love, Tim."

How that note and gift from a son, who so much yet needed her, touched Mom's heart and urged her on even more to work hard at therapy and recovery! Her face and nose needed reconstruction and even breathing was a challenge. How do you cry and wipe the tears and your nose while healing from such wounds?

When Mom finally came home from the hospital, she had a cute little pug nose, a nasal sound to her voice, and she walked with the help of crutches. The house still had only one bathroom and that was upstairs. The front living room was rearranged to improvise for all her needs until she could handle the long flight of stairs. Though her appearance and her voice had changed, the heart and soul of this wife and mother was the same. There was still a long road ahead for recovery, but life was beginning to feel right again in the McDowell household now that Mom was home.

COLLECTIONS OF THE HEART

stellamcdowell.com stellamcdowellauthor@gmail.com

COLLECTIONS OF THE HEART

The Stairway (excerpt)
by Dennis Knotts

CHAPTER ONE: THE FLIP OF A COIN

Rufus Riley stepped onto the wooden planks that made up the Chesapeake and Ohio railway station. The sign hanging over the platform read: Kanawha Valley. It was covered in soot from the continual passing of the locomotives belching smoke as they passed through. Unlike the train station, he had dressed in his best. He wore a suit and tie. He had polished his old shoes until they shined, and he had even managed to cover most of the scuff marks that had developed from his years of working in them.

His father had been a house painter, and Rufus Riley had the painting in his blood. However, there was also a mixture of adventure slipped in with the paint and turpentine. He had wanted to make a fresh start. This was now his life, and not his father's. Endless possibilities loomed before him.

COLLECTIONS OF THE HEART

Unfortunately, he had only one suit and one tie – and only one pair of shoes. He had always tried to keep his shoes clean, but at the end of each day, there were flecks of paint and several drops that had spattered during his workday with his father.

At night, he would take the single-edge razor blades they used to scrape paint off of windowpanes, and he would spend an hour or more removing all evidence of the paint and the splatters. But over the years, the color had come off the leather with the sharp edge of the blade. He had invested fifty cents for the black shoe dye and beamed with pride when the scratches and scuffs were hidden beneath the ebony liquid.

He had packed what few things he would need in an old suitcase once owned by his father and had set out for the railway station. He wanted to look his best and wanted his new life to be free from any clues of his past as he hoped that he would become the person he wanted to be, and not the person his past had dictated.

It suddenly dawned on him that he had no idea where he would go. He had a limited amount of cash in his pocket and knew not to travel far, but he needed a new place to start. He flagged down a stranger passing by,

"Excuse me, sir?" he inquired.

COLLECTIONS OF THE HEART

The man looked annoyed, but stopped all the same, "Yes?"

"Can you give me the name of a city?"

"A city?"

"Yes, I'm trying to figure out where I want to go."

"You'd be better off making a list of pros and cons of several cities," the stranger suggested and looked a little less annoyed. "That would be the sensible thing to do."

"I know, but I'm looking for a new life and an adventure..." he suggested.

"So, you're going to take the first city someone mentions and head there?"

"No," he admitted. He dug into his pocket and pulled out a quarter. "I'm going to get two names and flip a coin. I'll let destiny select my fate. What could be more adventurous than that?"

"Los Angeles," the stranger suggested. The look on Rufus' face made the stranger stop before moving on. "Too far?"

COLLECTIONS OF THE HEART

Rufus nodded. The stranger looked at the suit and noted that it was old and surmised Rufus was trying to make a clean break with his past. He remembered a day many years ago when he had the same adventure flowing through his veins. He thought for a minute and gave serious consideration to the request.

"Cincinnati," the stranger said. The stranger then flagged another man passing by. "Give us the name of a city."

"Name of a city?" he asked. "Is this a contest or a game?"

"No, this young man here is looking for two cities. He is then going to flip a coin and whichever city the coin selects, that's there he'll go for a fresh start."

"Sounds like someone is looking for an adventure. Alright. I'll bite. How about Baltimore?"

"Good," Rufus chimed. "So, if it's heads, I go to Baltimore; and if it's tails, I go to Cincinnati." As he made his announcement, both strangers stopped to see the result of his choice. The quarter spun into the air and rose five feet, six feet, eight feet. Rufus suddenly feared it might have been tossed too high and it might get lost. The two strangers motioned for other passers-by to step back so they could see

COLLECTIONS OF THE HEART

the quarter hit. Several asked what they were doing. The first stranger explained.

"Heads!" the second stranger declared. "Baltimore."

The reality of his decision struck home. "Wow! That's a pretty big decision to trust to a single flip of the coin," Rufus suggested.

"Best two out of three," the first stranger encouraged. Others had now gathered to see what was happening.

Rufus picked up the quarter and flipped it a second time, this time taking care not to put too much effort into it. Everyone watched the quarter spin wildly in the air and stepped back as it bounced, rolled, and finally settled on the wooden planks.

"Heads again!" someone in the crowd called out.

Rufus picked up the quarter and looked at the two strangers he had asked. They saw the look in his eyes. "Three out of five?" someone in the crowd suggested.

After ten tosses into the air, the first stranger picked up the quarter. He turned it over several times and examined both sides of the coin.

"What are you doing?" Rufus asked.

COLLECTIONS OF THE HEART

"Just making sure someone hadn't slipped in a two-headed quarter. I hear some places make them as a gag."

"Ten straight flips and ten *heads*," the second stranger observed. "That would be the logical explanation," he suggested.

Rufus looked at the first stranger as he handed the quarter back to him. "You toss it for me."

"Are you sure?" the stranger asked. Rufus nodded. The stranger flicked the coin into the air. All thirty-seven spectators who had gathered were holding their breath. The coin hit. It bounced. It rolled. It tottered like a dying top. It finally came to rest. No one said a word. They all looked at Rufus. He came over and looked down at the coin that controlled his destiny.

"Heads?" he gasped. The crowd began to break up. The first stranger patted him on the shoulder.

"Looks like someone wants you to go to Baltimore. Take my advice and go to Baltimore. It's not wise to anger the gods when they give you this kind of message."

"Rufus stooped down and picked up the coin. Everyone had moved on. He looked at the coin, and then he looked up into the sky and asked, "Yes, but which God?"

COLLECTIONS OF THE HEART

TODAY, THY NAME IS GRACE
by Cindy Tesar

"My grace is sufficient for thee. My strength is made perfect in weakness."   2 Corinthians 12:9

Sixteen is such sweet naivety, the emergence of the butterfly from her chrysalis, dewy fresh and barely able to fly. She took the car and her new license for a solo flight to no destination in particular other than to test the wings of adulthood. Local streets were pretty calm as she drove past the strip malls and the park. Turning down the expressway and finding only a trio of cars, she merged and reached to set the radio to her pop/alternative universe. She unleashed the uncontrollable urge to tap along to the beat of the captivating music. Soon her foot pressed on the accelerator, taking 40 mph up to 50 as she zoomed into the curve. Just on the edge of scary/feeling good, her stomach did a little flip of thrill. Suddenly, the car ahead put on its brakes. *No problem!* She swerved to the right-hand lane to go around the pokey car. It was then that she spied the little dog crossing in the road.

Just in time, she was able to gun it and avoid both the car and the pup. *Close call!* Scared her a bit, but she reigned in her speed as her heart threatened to beat out of her chest. For the next few miles, she held it at 35 mph and soon arrived at the other side of town.

She pulled into the DQ drive-thru and ordered a chocolate-dipped cone, her favorite. So, adult, it was to order from the left side of the car and pull forward to the pick-up and pay. The girl handed the cone through the window, accompanied by a stack of napkins. Small beads of vanilla ice cream began to leak from underneath the chocolate shell cap. She licked them and wrapped the base in a couple of napkins to catch future drips. Still slurping at the cone, she barely missed a little girl who had broken free of her mother's hand in the parking lot. She stopped. It was a convenient time to get in another few licks as mother and child were reunited. Continuing across the parking lot to the driveway, she turned one-handed into the street, but the wheel came loose from her grip, and she nearly collided with the car in the other lane. Once completing the turn, again, she aggressively licked at her treat, and the whole cap came off, falling to her lap. She only glanced down for a nano-second, and *whoa!* she nearly landed in the bed of the truck ahead, stopped at the light. Again, she welcomed the little time-out to encase the ball of ice cream and wad the whole mess in the remaining napkins. The light changed just as her phone rang. It's as though her best friend could read her thoughts.

"Hi!"

"Hi, back!"

"Guess who got her license today?"

"That's dope! (which is teen-talk for something really good)."

"Wait, I'll send you a *selfie*..." With that, she scrolled to the icon, posed, and pressed send just as the red lights flashed behind her.

Oh, NO!! What do I do?

She pulled to the curb just as an ambulance came screaming across the intersection. *Didn't see that coming.*

He walked to the window as she rolled it down. "License and registration, he demanded sternly. "Do you know why I pulled you over?"

"No, sir."

"State law says no handheld devices may be used while operating a motor vehicle. Distracted driving. Failure to yield to an oncoming emergency vehicle."

She leaned across to the glove box to retrieve the registration and then dug through her purse that had slipped to the floor next to the balled-up ice cream mess. *Mean cop! Buzzkill!*

Surrendering the paper-work, she gulped, but it was too late. Meltdown had begun, and the tears came.

Looking over the requested items, he asked, "How long have you had your license?"

"Got it today," she muttered through a sob.

He let her squirm awhile before speaking again. "I should write you up, but I'm going to let you off with a warning. If you want to live and drive another day, there will be no more selfies or talking on the phone. And, Missy, sirens, and lights should make you stop and take notice. Maybe lower the tunes, okay? Got it?"

"She nodded

"And…wipe the chocolate off your face. It doesn't match the pretty girl on your photo."

COLLECTIONS OF THE HEART

She sniffled, wiped, and managed a weak smile. He tapped on the roof of her car as he turned to rejoin his cruiser.

She spoke out loud, "Adult-ing is so hard!" Calmly, she replaced her license and registration. The car started with a purr, and she headed home, hyper-alert, and vigilant. She was in full control now, or so she thought. *The dog…it could happen to anyone; the girl in the parking lot…the other car…the fallen cone…the ambulance…the cop stop.* That was an impressive list of close calls, nearlies, almosts, and just-in-times. Things could have ended much differently.

Perhaps it was the glint through the windshield in the afternoon sun, but she would swear there was someone sitting next to her as co-pilot. There was a sudden warm feeling in the pit of her stomach, a peaceful calm. Grace had made herself known.

2018

POEMS

COLLECTIONS OF THE HEART

A Child's Conversation with God
by Sharon Miller

There they go again – arguing and fighting night after night.
   If they really love each other, why do they often fight?
   I cannot understand why they're so angry and uptight.

   If it gets worse, I'll have to pray they divorce each other.
   Make them obey Your commandment to love one another.
   Help them to love like every good father and mother.

   If they divorce, that will stop the yelling.
   But who will I live with, and where will the other be dwelling?
   Would I see them both? Would the anger stop?-no telling.

Don't they care that their fighting confuses and fills us with dread?
A curfew on their anger would give us the peace to sleep instead.
If we can't fight, why can't children send fighting parents to

COLLECTIONS OF THE HEART

bed?

Ephesians 4:31-32; 5:1-2 All bitterness, anger, and wrath, shouting and slander must be removed from you, along with all malice. And be kind and compassionate to one another, forgiving one another, just as God also forgave you in Christ. Therefore, be imitators of God, as dearly loved children. And walk in love, as the Messiah also loved us and gave Himself for us, a sacrificial and fragrant offering to God.

ALONE
by Sharon Miller

Today, like many others, I ventured outside to play.
As was my custom, I stood at the edge of the driveway.
Then that fear rose up inside me that I'd be sent away.
So, I gave up and went home before anyone could say
Anything that would make me feel any more - alone.

I used to go to Ginger's house- with fear I'd ring the bell.
I never knew whether she'd let me in or if she'd tell
Me to go away because she was with a friend so swell
There wasn't any reason for them to play with me as well
And I'd have to make that long walk back home - alone.

And so, I stood outside the home of the family Leake

I chose their home- I decided to take another peek.
I wanted to get up enough courage for me to speak.
And thereby, I was hoping to get what I always seek-
Someone to be a friend so I wouldn't be left - alone.

But I couldn't ever imagine they would answer the door.
Let alone, ask me to come in to play- which I would adore
Without a doubt, I knew what end I would receive in store
To be sent home again-that would surely hurt to my core.
I'd rather not have to go through that once more – alone.

I never felt alone inside the pages of any book.
Books can't reject you – they always beckon you to look.
"Come inside," they call to you from some comfortable nook.
"Come enjoy some adventure instead of being forsook.
So, my books were a better alternative to being - alone.

A few days, I did have fun times with friends out and about.
I don't know why my imagination filled me with doubt.
But other times my fears were confirmed when they did play out.
Then that revolting feeling inside of me made me pout.
It wasn't worth the effort, so I stayed - alone.

I needed someone to realize how afraid I was.
COLLECTIONS OF THE HEART

And make the effort to be a friend- as one always does.
If they would only come out with a wave and a smile because-
I was waiting to be invited to play without fuss.
Surely then I'd have ignored my fear of being - alone

If you see a someone standing alone at your driveway's edge,
Please take just a moment to come out on your own porch ledge.
Give them a wave and an invitation to serve as a pledge
Of friendship and encouragement instead of to dredge
up the fear that would make them believe they're – alone.

Romans 12:10, 13, 15-16, 18 Show family affection to one another with brotherly love.
Outdo one another in showing honor. Share with the saints in their needs;
pursue hospitality. Rejoice with those who rejoice.;
weep with those who weep. Be of the same mind with one another.

COLLECTIONS OF THE HEART

An Ode to Ease the Bereft
by Sharon Miller

Almighty God, you know I love you with all that I am.
But this loss makes me doubt and fear.
I cannot understand how You could take so soon
This loved one whom I hold so dear.

There are many people all around me
Yet still I feel so all alone.
Why did You take my dear one from me?
I fear my broken heart will turn to stone.

May it never be- I beg of You
That my grief should turn me cold.
I know my dear one is better off
As Your presence and glory unfold.

Caress my wandering thoughts, O LORD
Keep them pure, admirable, lovely and true.
Infuse my heart with peace and contentment
As only You can and will to do.

COLLECTIONS OF THE HEART

Please vanquish any bitterness and doubt
that would tarnish the love You offer me.
And fill me with the beauties of my friend
Until we are side by side for eternity.

Almighty God, you know I love you with all that I am
Holy Spirit hover over me, Jesus hold my hand.
Help me overcome my loneliness
I am a little wobbly now as I walk this land.

COLLECTIONS OF THE HEART

A Christian Writer's Prayer
by Sharon Miller

Then the LORD answered me and said, "Write down the vision;
Make it plain on tablets, so that the one who reads it may run.
For the vision is a witness for the appointed time to be done;
A testimony to the end; it will not disappoint anyone.

If it delays, wait for it – it will not be late, it will surely come.
Habakkuk 2: 2,3 (NASBRE)

Dear LORD,

I thank You for the gift you gave me –
The one for which I was born and bred.
Words flow into sentences,
All dancing in rhyme and prose inside my head.
I can't keep them all pent up –
They must tumble out on my tablet instead.
But what did You mean for me to do
And to whom should they be said?

I want to give courage

And hope to children weighed down.
Yet, how can I help others
When my life keeps sputtering around?

I haven't always been "salt and light" - mostly,
I've been lost not found.

So how can I help others "taste and see"
All the good that does abound?
You, my Father, always know best –
You gave me this wonderful treasure.

All that I need to complete the vision
You have given me in full measure.
I'll steadily work on the vision
While I wait on Your lead to make sure
That I write your pure thoughts
To show the distressed Your good pleasure.

What would You have me to say, LORD?
And who are the ones waiting to hear?
COLLECTIONS OF THE HEART

Does my vision come from You, LORD?
Is it encouraging and clear?

What have I to offer that no one else can?
Oh LORD, please lend me your ear.
Make the vision I've worked diligently on,
Erase their pain, or give them cheer.
AMEN

BRIEF THOUGHTS ON SIMON OF CYRENE
by Dennis Knotts

You stood there on the sidelines, carefree,

As that One went past to His destiny.

But what were your thoughts that day

As the Son of God was led away?

Some said you followed Him before,

Others said you were unsure.

Or did you want it all to be done

Never having seen God's Son?

But whatever your mood that day

You were chosen for a role to play.

As Jesus did stumble in the street

Your own destiny you did meet.

You carried the cross for Christ that day

When His last strength had ebbed away.

You helped Him on to His ultimate goal

And that was just to save your soul.

Dear Father, I wish I could have been the one

Who stooped to help Your exhausted Son.

If only I could have eased His load

And helped Him on down along the road.

COLLECTIONS OF THE HEART

"I have a cross for you as well.
Made for the time and place you dwell."
"But Father, it's hard; and none have seen.
I'd rather have been Simon of Cyrene."
"A cross is a load that you must bear
But I will help you, to be fair.
Carry your cross, as Simon did mine
And I will help you to bear thine."
"But You needed Simon on that day,
Or Your mission would have died along the way."
"And what of here? What of now?
Who'll do my work, or even know how?"
I stood shocked at my thoughts of pride.
I wanted to serve God with praise beside.
Simon, you helped Him when none would praise
Since you had no knowledge of these latter days.

So why must I serve Him while others can see?
Am I drawing praise only to me?
O Father, forgive me, and change my ways
And let me serve You unnoticed all of my days.
--Knotts—

COLLECTIONS OF THE HEART

GIVE
by Sharon Miller

When push comes to shove,
There's not enough love
For each child to go 'round.
So many are left out
All they can do is shout
cause tears don't make a sound.

But most have no voice
They're not given a choice
In what happens in their life.
They are bounced here and there
Made to feel no one cares
They receive strife upon strife.

Is it any wonder
psyches torn asunder
produce adults that aren't whole?
Some stand and fight in fear.
Others spread the nightmare
to their kids who bear the toll.

Some hold their dreams so tight
They stand again to fight
And finally, they get there.
But in that cold system
Most need someone to be with them -
A mentor to guide them somewhere.

So much needs to be done
We need you, me, everyone
To lift them and help them stand.

COLLECTIONS OF THE HEART

Whatever you do best
Make it your personal quest
To help kids hurt in this land.

"We who are strong have an obligation to bear with the weaknesses of those without strength, and not to please ourselves. Each one of us must please his neighbor for his good, to build him up." Romans 15:1-2 HCSB

Harried
by Stella McDowell

I check the clock, no time to spare.

I grab my last clean pants to wear.

It's time to leave I do declare

I have no time to fix my hair.

Why do I live in disrepair?

Why don't I learn to just prepare?

And start the day with sunrise air

And make the time for praise and prayer.

Then days like this might be more rare

And I'd have time to fix my hair.

Hearts That Touch
by Merry Streeter

Loving gestures, a smile from some,
Lifts the weight of one undone,
Understanding ways, gentle tongue,
Soothes the soreness of tattered young,

Soft eyes gleaming warmth with care,
Oh, to catch it, and somehow share,
Tenderness, listening ears,
Will they stay or shall I fear,
The empty space with no one dear,

Oh, how I want to draw near
To hearts unfurled, not closed and tight,
Seeking truth and all that's right,
Embrace the moment of hearts that touch,
With equal taste for light and…

Much is given, much is gained,
Even in the course of pain,
If I can be with those that want
Exchange of thoughts and not to taunt
My depths with outward show;
I will be satisfied; I will grow.

HURTFUL WORDS
by Sharon Miller

"Sticks and stones may break your bones
but words can never hurt you"
Couldn't be further from the truth.
Broken bones take time to heal
but oh, the damage words can deal -
They continue to prick not soothe.

When hurtful words enter the mind
It's rare for them just to play through.
They banter about and twist and shout
Until your soul feels black and blue.
They continue without leaving a
Then only many kind words can subdue.

Why do people get away with hurling
words that they know will hurt?
If each word was assessed a fee
People might think before they blurt.
If kind words could earn them some cash

perhaps more kindness they'd exert.

Sometimes people say their words
were spoken only in fun.

But each word needs to be measured
by the damage that is done.
One needs to use encouraging words
or let their words be none.

"A soothing tongue (speaking words that build up and encourage) is a tree of life.
But a perversive tongue (speaking words that overwhelm and depress) crushes the spirit."
Proverbs 15:4 AMP

COLLECTIONS OF THE HEART

The Encounter
by Cindy Tesar

It was your laughter first caught my ear,

infectious like a child at play.

A sonic avalanche splashed my face with exhilarating joy.

You, flirtatious creature, You!

The stormy blue of your eyes flashes to a sunny twinkle in the passing of clouds.

I reach for you with unsure footing,

yet it is You who slip through my grasp.

We converse for hours, yet never meet at minds, for we cannot.

I attempt to rise above your effervescence, but you shout me down.

My anxieties are swept away in your babble, eclipsing every argument in the stones of your truth.

I am serious!

You are driven by an unseen force taking turns and dodges at will as though chased. You make it a game!

We fished together, You and I,

my pursuit for food and yours as catch and release.

COLLECTIONS OF THE HEART

Only cautious approach can I come lest
I be swept into Your insanity.

Drenched in love I shiver breathed upon by the wind

And doff my shoes to stand upon holy ground.
Speak to me, O Mighty River of God!

My Heart's A Fraud
by Merry Streeter

We go about our day to day,
Folk looking for what's right,
At times we fail and lose our way,
Although God's ways are bright.

"I'll follow my heart!" I hear some say,
With glee that makes them smile,
But woe to them, for on this day
The heart will soon beguile,

Fraught with blarney and boondoggle,
Duplicity lies in wait,
While wanting joy and happiness,
Sometimes we're tricked by bait.

"What shall we do?" I hear some say,
If truth the heart's a fraud,
The Spirit says, "Just follow Me.
I'll show the road not flawed."

COLLECTIONS OF THE HEART

The Word of God is light enough,
To guide a seeking heart.

It's light and prudence for that path
To make one wise and sharp.

So be assured God's ways are good,
Trustworthy all the same,
So, hope and know the path is straight
If pleasing Him's your aim

THE UNSEEN HEART
by Cindy Tesar

And so, it begins…

Drawn from God's mysterious treasury

A spark, a flash, a flicker of life

Keeping time with the Maestro's beat

Ba-boomp, ba-boomp, the first sonic detections

A rhythm from the unseen realm

Birth, out of darkness and into the light

Present, yet unseen, yet bearing *imageo dei*

Carrying eternity's life, purpose, and giftedness

And the beat goes on…

3, 300, 000, 000 incredible times in the average 80-year span

It quickens with love, exercise, or in the face of danger

Yet sleeps in heavenly peace all through the night

Ba-boomp, ba-boomp…ba-boomp…

Pledged in love, rising courageously amidst conflict

Tender and full of pity, yet hardened against untruth

Broken, bereft, yet resilient

Through many dangers, toils, and snares

And the beat goes on…

To mark the time, keep the pace, run the race

Upward to join the high calling

To join the Father's dance

To beat again, heart to heart, with Him for eternity.

May we NEVER stop a beating heart!

Cindy Tesar@ 2019

The Walls Of My Life
by Dennis Knotts

The walls of my life –

I had been so proud of the walls of my life.

I had put all my efforts into them,

They were the best that I could build;

High and strong they were.

I could make none better.

And so I sat down

Secure

In the walls of my life.

And as I sat, there came a gentle tapping

And my walls began to shake.

They broke apart and crumbled

And when I dug myself out of the debris

There stood Satan

Who had touched the walls

And made them fall.

I gathered the remains of my wall

And stacked them back up,

But he leaned on them and they fell once more.

And so my life became a nightmare

Of trying to build a wall for protection

Between Satan and myself,

And watching how easy it was

For him to knock it down.

And then You came along, Lord,

And offered to help.

When I accepted, to my horror

You picked up all my bricks

And threw them away;

So now there was nothing

Between Satan and me

COLLECTIONS OF THE HEART

But You.

And then You knelt and drew a circle around me;

A pencil-thin line of crimson –

A circle of Your blood.

And Satan tried to advance,

But could not;

And he stood without,

Beating and howling

And throwing himself in rage

Against that pencil-thin crimson line;

And I came to understand

What is truly meant

To trust

In God.

THUG
by Cindy Tesar

A THUG CAME BY THE OTHER DAY

MESSING WITH MY PEACE

HE TWISTED EVERY WORD I SAID

AND WOULD NOT GIVE RELEASE

REMINDED I'D BEEN DEPUTIZED

AT ONE I STOOD MY GROUND

SLAMMED HIM UP AGAINST MY CAR

SO HE COULDN'T MAKE A SOUND

I CUFFED HIM AND LED HIM OFF

WARNED HIM ONCE OR TWICE

HE MUST NOT PASS THIS WAY AGAIN

I HAVE THE MIND OF CHRIST!

COLLECTIONS OF THE HEART

2 Corinthians 10:5b KJV

"...and take every thought captive to the obedience of Christ."

TO WHOM IT MAY CONCERN
by Sharon Miller

To whom it may concern:
Before I venture out on my own
I have a lot I need to learn
from being a child to being grown.

You see I have a future to fulfill
And I'm filled with many hopes.
I just need someone nearby until
I can figure out the ropes.

My parents aren't here for me
They are living with their mistakes.
How can I become all I can be
if they don't have what it takes?

The judge placed me in a new family
with some people I don't know.
They give me food, clothes and things I need
but I can't tell if they are friend or foe.

COLLECTIONS OF THE HEART

Following rules are important, it seems.
If I do, they are friendly and kind.
But I can't always follow their routines.
Then they react and blow my mind.

And so, I thought I'd write this ode
"To whom it may concern,"
I'll need some help along life's road
to get what I need to learn.

Romans 15:1-2 "Now we who are strong have an obligation
to
bear the weaknesses of those without strength,
and not to please ourselves. Each one of us must please his
neighbor
for his good, to build him up."
Proverbs 22:6 "Train up a child in the way he should go;
even when he is old, he will not depart from it."

COLLECTIONS OF THE HEART

SWEET SALLY BROWN
by Cindy Tesar

There once was a girl named Sweet Sally Brown

Whose face wore a frown turned upside-down

A girl of contradictions

Unpredictable prediction

A lady fair with the heart of a clown.

She drank her wine before it was time

From grapes that clung to the vine.

Like a child with no brain

She danced in the rain.

Spouting poetry that never did rhyme

She toted an umbrella each day in the sun

And assessed daily drudgery as nothing but fun.

When work called her name

She made it a game.

Gave away all her money and proclaimed, "It is done!"

COLLECTIONS OF THE HEART

She answered all questions before they were asked.

And did all her chores before they were tasked.

They thought she was crazy

A daffodil daisy.

Her face made-up was unmasked.

The workers around her would say, "We're all done!"

She clapped her hands saying, "We've only begun!"

A girl of contradictions

Unpredictable predictions

An enigma, a puzzle, and wrapped up in fun!

DEVOTIONALS

FIRE IN THE HOLE
by Cindy Tesar

-THE DYNAMITE OF GOD-

Commonly used in mountain-moving projects or mining, dynamite is a blasting agent detonated in amounts proportionate to a given project. In the old days, before electrical charges were employed, a runner would strap sticks of dynamite together around a central fuse, stick it in a blasting hole, light the fuse, and run like…well, really fast, yelling "Fire in the Hole!" It was a warning that there might be debris flying from an impending blast, lit and ready to blow.

Railroads, intent upon expanding their territories, blasted mountains that obstructed laying of their tracks. Miners, too, would blast away a rocky mountain if they saw that a certain formation indicated there was a seam of gold. It gave them access to the true treasures of the earth.

The Greek word DUNAMIS, from which we get dynamite, is defined as (miraculous) power, might, or strength. It is often used in scripture to speak of endowments of the Holy Spirit. Christians are familiar with Pentecost, the gift of the Holy Spirit, that came upon those gathered in the Upper Room after Jesus departed for heaven. Pentecost, fifty days after the Resurrection, was the *fire in the hole* for the church. We saw the birth of the church, going forth on fire and demonstrating the power of a Mighty God. Just as Jesus performed miracles by the *dynamite* of God, so the *fire* was passed to the early church.

On the road to Emmaus, Jesus disclosed scriptures to men. Though they did not recognize Him they did say, "Did not our hearts *burn* within us?" (Luke 24:32) We are urged to keep our lamps *burning* (Luke 12:35) The zeal to serve God, empowered by His Holy Spirit, should be like a *fire in the belly*. We're cautioned not to quench the *fire* of the Holy Spirit. (1 Thessalonians 5:19) Let your light shine!

As we face the evil days of darkness in the end times, we need even more of the power of God to combat the principalities and powers who seek to destroy us.

2 Corinthians 10:4 "For the weapons of our warfare are not physical (weapons of flesh and blood), but they are MIGHTY before God for the overthrow and destruction of strongholds…" [emphasis, mine, on the MIGHTY, dynamite of God]

COLLECTIONS OF THE HEART

As we pray for our families, our community, our nation, and the volatile worldwide situations, may we employ the *dunamis* of the Holy Spirit to do battle. There may be flying debris as we endeavor to lay new inroads for the kingdom of God or to mine out the rich treasures of scripture. May we venture forth with His fire in our bellies and as we do, sound the warning, "Fire in the Hole!"

Seize the day in Jesus' Name and in the power of His might! (dyna-might)

Blessings!

"…Give Me This Mountain…"
by Dennis Knotts

Joshua 14:12:

"Now, therefore, give me this mountain, whereof the Lord spoke in that day; for you heard in that day how the Anakims were there, and that the cities were great and fenced: if so be the Lord will be with me, then I shall be able to drive them out, as the Lord said."

I love Caleb. I want my life to be a mirror image of Caleb. He served God. God made a promise to him. He had to wait forty years before they entered the land. He had to wait until most of the conquest was done. As the land was being divided up, Caleb came to Joshua with this request.

For those of you who skipped Sunday School that day, Moses sent in twelve spies to go into the Promised Land and check it out. The twelve spies came back with their report. Ten of the spies focused on the giants in the land and not the promise of God. Joshua and Caleb focused on the power of God and not the obstacles before them. The Children of Israel followed the ten spies. They gave in to fear and surrendered their faith. God punished the Children of Israel and no one over twenty years of age – except for Joshua and Caleb – would be allowed to go into the Promised Land.

Caleb was forty years old when he went into the Promised Land to spy on it for Moses. They were forty more years in the Wilderness. He was eighty when they entered the Promised Land and this scene is after the conquest. Moses had promised Caleb the mountain called Hebron. This city was filled with giants. That is what Anakims are – they are Nephilim giants. It was a fortified city filled with giants. He was over eighty years old, and he wanted to go in and take it.

The Children of Israel gave in to fear. They followed popular opinion. They feared and because they feared they surrendered their faith in God. Because they gave in to fear, God could not bless them. They lost what God had promised.

COLLECTIONS OF THE HEART

I never want to be like them. I never want to give in to fear. I never want to follow the majority. There is a mountain out there which will have my name on it. I know that it is not an easy mountain to take. I know Satan has fortified it with giants of his own all to keep me from going forth.

But this is my prayer to God today: "Lord, give me this mountain." I know in my own strength I cannot take the mountain. But I know my God can do all things. I know that God can defeat the enemy for me. I know that God determines who the victor will be in any battle. And so I trust God to give it to me. No matter how old I am when the battle starts; I know God will give me the victory. The stronger the enemy, the greater the victory over them.

And so I look at the mountain. I am not even sure what this mountain will mean in my life or God's Plan, but I want this mountain because Satan is trying to keep it from me. I want this mountain, not for personal glory. But I want this mountain so I can point at my God and shout to the world: "He did this for me!" I want the world to see how great my God truly is. I want God to give me this mountain so that the world will know that He exists and that He is greater than any opposition.

And so I cry out to God this day, "Lord, give me this mountain."

Is there a mountain in your future? Has God promised you a mountain that is impossible to obtain? Do not give in to fear. Do not follow the majority. Be the one who cries out to God, "Give me this mountain." And let's see what God can do with those who are willing to trust Him and follow Him.

--Dennis Knotts—

© Copyright 2020 The Fred List

Used with permission. All rights reserved

God Dispenses the Wind
by Phyllis Boles

You lift me up to the wind and cause me to ride, And You dissolve me in a storm. Job 30:22

While visiting the beach and stopping for a bite to eat, I watch sailboats ride the waves. Turning, I notice a one-legged seagull standing on a boardwalk post. Its left foot seems to be cut off at the knee, resembling a stick. The wind whistles through the air and captures me with its strong gusts. I look at the seagull. In turn, it looks at me unfazed by the strength of the winds coming from the ocean. I pull my jacket close to my body, yet the seagull stands firm on one leg, unmoved by the winds as if it's a regular occurrence.

Like the seagull, God gives us the strength to stand as He draws us close to him, clothing us with his strength and (standing like the seagull shows strength, thought it would be good to include it) protection. He lifts us in the storms when it seems everything is pulled away from under us. When it seems as if we only have one leg to stand on, His protection is perfect for the winds that come.

God equips us to stand even with our cumbersome hindrances. Many times we feel as if we have one leg to stand on, especially when the winds come to knock us down. God's design for us in the storm is to lose any ties that bind us to earthly matters.

Strong winds loosen the debris holding on to our souls. Winds show up to consume our fears and failures. For God's children, winds often come as cyclones but are not designed to draw us into tunnels of darkness. If God is the one who dispenses the wind, will he leave us to its destruction? No, God equips us through the storms of life.

March ends the winter season and, at the same time, begins the spring season. These two seasons strike against one another with forceful impacting winds. The harsh winds at the beginning of the month gradually release their grip to give way to the milder winds at the end of the month. As March comes in like a lion and goes out like a lamb, in much the same way, God brings the harsh winds then leads us to the soft, gentle breezes after the storms.

In God's gentle breeze, we are changed for the good or the bad as a result of the winds. We can allow the winds of our circumstances to blow lies of sand in our eyes so we can't see the truth. We can allow the winds to dry out fruit on the vine, so we don't grow to maturity in Christ. Or we can allow the fresh winds of God's Spirit, no matter how harsh, shape us by allowing the winds to erode our rough surfaces. It's our choice.

Even in the winds, the seagull can stand strong or fly away. We, too, can stand strong during storms, but running away is not a good option.

COLLECTIONS OF THE HEART

The gentle winds come surely as our seasons change. As the cold harsh winds give way to the warm, gentle breezes, erosion in our soul gives way to new growth. A new season begins. We flourish and fly with new breath in our lungs, fresh courage in our hearts, and renewed hope in our spirit. We don't depend on our two legs or even one leg to stand in the storm. We depend on the fresh wind of God's Spirit to sweep us off our feet and are not given over to destruction.

Yet on this day, God's creation displays to me His majesty. God can lift me above the gusts, even with the hindrance of one leg. The glory of His majesty is watching the seagull fly away no longer agitated by the winds - a beautiful sight to behold. When God lifts me up to fly on the winds of His wings, all substance attempting to weigh me down drifts away. And I soar to new heights.

God Will Defend Me!
by Merry Streeter

Therefore this is what the LORD says: "See, I will defend your cause and avenge you...Jeremiah 51:36a

Trying out for the drill team was very exciting! My best friend Mary and I couldn't wait to get to the meeting and hear what we needed to do. After school, though, I couldn't find her but went ahead to the gathering. After tryouts and learning that I made the team, I went to look for my friend. Going to her house and knocking on the door, her mother let me in with a scowl. She ordered me to sit in the kitchen; I wondered why her mom was so abrupt, but I overheard from Mary's bedroom:

"Merry is probably lying for you!" I heard my friend's mother say. *What!? I don't lie!* Her words from the back bedroom hit me like a brick, and I felt heat rise to my head. I began to stand up to march to her room and let her mom know I don't lie, when a firm and solemn voice spoke to my mind, "Sit down, you don't need to defend yourself." Stunned, I slowly sat down, recognizing it was the voice of my Lord. He was directing to keep me from doing something that didn't please

Him. I knew He was teaching me, and I marveled at His voice, loving and firm at the same time. Jesus filled my heart and quieted my spirit. I could only sit in wonder and awe at what had just happened. I don't know what happened to Mary, but I went home, having grown in the Lord a little more.

It was a new experience since I was a baby-Christian, and it wouldn't be the last. *I don't need to defend myself, the Lord said. He would protect me*—what a tremendous promise.

Lord, You are an excellent teacher. You fully understand what level of maturity we're at and treat us accordingly. You teach us your ways and how to conduct ourselves. You teach us in Your Word just like you taught Jeremiah. And just as Jesus was silent when Herod of Antipas hurled accusations and questions at him to get him to defend himself, I don't need to defend myself either. You are my vindicator. Thank you for being there for me. Amen.

COLLECTIONS OF THE HEART

"I See You in Everything All Day"
by Reina Dozier

Father, I want to be honest with You. I want to be real. I have been thinking, for a non-believer it is easy to say, "Where is your God now?" But for a Christ-follower, it is very hard to say, "Where is God in this?" We know He is there. Yet we look at the world around us and think, man, what has this world come to? There are diseases and disorder; chaos and conflict. Sodom and Gomorrah would blush at what the world is doing now! There is a law that just passed in New York stating that as long as a woman hasn't started contractions, it is okay for them to kill their baby and call it abortion! When you fill out paperwork at a county hospital, it no longer asks if you are male or female. They ask you what gender do you associate.

Schools are getting shot up, buildings getting blown up, and perverts lurking behind the faces of your everyday people; teachers, managers, your next-door neighbor. Little Susie hides the secret of Uncle Joe. There are death and destruction on every news channel you flip through. Then there are the natural disasters, hurricanes, tsunamis, earthquakes, fires, tornados, storms, oceans raging, dry vegetation blazing, famine, political riots, death for being a Christian, sued for being a Christian! Our religious rights are being sniped away one by one by the wicked one. Oh God, is it so hard to ask where are You in all of this! I know You are there, but where?

I'm on my knees face down, crying over what this world has come to? Then I feel a gentle hand upon my chin lifting my face. The corner of a robe wipes my tears away. I see the Light before me, soft but radiant. I get my eyes focused back on my Savior, my Creator, my Daddy. I hear that still, small Voice assure me, "I am there." I am there in the arms of a passer by-er putting a blanket around a homeless man. I am there in the words of a prayer warrior whose heart breaks for the colony of tents sprung up in a dried-out riverbed underneath a bridge as she drives her husband to work. I am there in the testimony of the bullied, as well as the reformed bully. I am there behind a couch with a hiding child covering her ears because mommy and daddy are fighting again, and this time there is blood. All she hears is the sound of Angels singing. I am there in the raging ocean. I am there in the calm sea. I am there in the burnt arms of a fireman who ran back in for little Johnny's puppy. I am there in the words of a Pastor telling a broken down prostitute Jesus loves her. I am there in the silence of a drug addict who hit his rock bottom and is ready to look up. I am there on the mountain tops. I am there in the valley lows. I am aware and in control of the chaos. I am there in the government. I am there in the underground Churches. I am there at conception. I am there at death. I am there in the tears of a mother who can't find the words to comfort her daughter after a miscarriage. I am there in the prayers of a father whose child is victorious in putting their perpetrator behind bars. I am there in the strength of that father not to take justice in his very capable hands. I am there with the mentally challenged, emotionally challenged, and spiritually challenged. I am there."

Now with a smile, I brush off my knees, take a deep breath, and face the world around me. Suddenly the world looks different as I sing a little tune, "I see You in everything all day." I just might have an answer when the non-believer cries out, "Where is God now!" I love You, Jesus.

Let's Start Stacking.
by Merry Streeter

"...Each of you is to carry out a stone on your shoulder— twelve stones in all, one for each of the twelve tribes. We will use them to build a monument so that in the future, when your children ask, 'What is this monument for?' you can tell them, 'It is to remind us that the Jordan River stopped flowing when the Ark of God went across!' The monument will be a permanent reminder to the people of Israel of this amazing miracle." Joshua 4:5b-7 Living Bible

While strolling along a southern California rocky seashore, I was awed by the colored beauty strewn all along the coast like a mosaic. Each unique hue held a pattern of its own: one tan oblong, another blue oval, and thousands upon thousands of them. Stooping to stack some into a pile, I remembered how the children of Israel were commanded by God to stack rocks too. God wanted them to remember a great miracle He performed for them and to be able to answer their children's questions when asked why the stack was there in the first place. I wondered if I was able to remember all that God had done for me?

Aren't all our lives filled with God's interventions too? Can you recall them? Like stacking rocks, we need to compile those God-interventions either by journal, diary, photo, short stories, books, or even a memoir. And I pray our children and grandchildren will consider the memories and recall the stories of a powerful and interactive God; that they will know the God who made them is still alive and well and wants to be actively involved in their lives too.

Since we are blessed having seen Him work in our lives, and if we've passed that memory on to our children and our children's children, it might be the most important legacy we leave them! Let's start stacking!

COLLECTIONS OF THE HEART

Prayer: Lord, We love you and appreciate everything you have done. Please help us to create a memory of the beautiful things you have done in our lives. Amen.

Life Is A Vapor
by Merry Streeter

Come now, you who say, "Today or tomorrow we will go to such and such a city, and spend a year there and engage in business and make a profit." 14 [a]Yet you do not know [b]what your life will be like tomorrow. You are just a vapor that appears for a little while and then vanishes away.
James 4: 13-17

I once worked for Fox Photo in a kiosk very similar to what you see up here. The store, strategically placed in a parking lot where people could conveniently drive up and drop off their film for developing. It was ideal for people to leave their cartridges or rolls and later pick up their pictures en route to home or work.   How many of you remember these?

It was my second job and a welcome change from the Sub Sandwich/Donut Shop (about 50 yards from the kiosk) and was a perfect job for me then. Being a self-motivated individual, this allowed more excellent opportunity to share Christ uninterrupted during a lull, and privacy to read and pray in the spare time. This little store was awarded #1 in our district because we worked hard, kept up with our customers, kept it clean, and we were very good at customer service. I say," we," as it took two girls to work it. One morning girl (myself) and one afternoon girl, (my sister-in-law, Kathy) usually. We both loved being a light for Christ. At my shift, I also enjoyed bringing a Bible for devotions, so in my spare time, I could read and pray in this mini sanctuary.

I valued time with anyone who stayed a while, most often using it to share Christ face to face, one on one, until other customers came. In the afternoon, kids walked by going home from school. One kid, in particular, liked to come by and hang out a while and talk. He was an unkept gangly 13-year-old kid with long, waist-length dirty black hair, dirty clothes, and a guitar slung over his shoulder. He looked homeless, but he wasn't. This boy, Eddie, was often high and

COLLECTIONS OF THE HEART

notably without real purpose, so my concern for him was great.

At some point, he asked me not to talk to him anymore about Jesus, so I reluctantly agreed. Time passed, and on occasion, he'd stop to say hello. But after months passed, I became greatly concerned for his salvation, so much so I quietly cried out to the Lord for him.

Then one day, he came strolling by and stopped to say hello as he had done before. His eyes were floating; he was high again. The weight in my heart now overwhelming and unbearable I told him so. That I was VERY burdened for his soul, knowing that he could leave our conversation and maybe die that day. I told him I remembered agreeing not to mention Jesus anymore but felt such an urgency to bring Him up again. I asked if he even knew where he was going if he should die? He listened carefully and didn't object this time. I asked him, "If Jesus came and stood right next to you, looked you right in the eyes with His amazing love, and asked if you'd go with him; would you go?" Much to my surprise, he said, "Yes." Shocked but pleased, I asked him to pray with me, and he agreed. Taking his hands, I prayed with him. After leading him in the sinner's prayer, he lifted his eyes to look at me, no longer foggy or floating, but clear,

COLLECTIONS OF THE HEART

bright, and sound, much like the eyes of another young man who had a God encounter with me.

Eddie smiled, "I feel different!" he said, touching his chest. We both smiled. I told him, " The Bible says when one person comes to the Lord, the angels in heaven rejoice!" He liked that. He left, but I was still rejoicing! That made my day!

Later that same day, I learned from one of his friends, he hopped on a motorcycle with a friend for a ride and was killed instantly in a collision! I sat frozen, taking it in. Now the whole burden and sense of urgency made perfect sense. I was sad he was gone but so relieved that he finally opened his heart to Jesus in the nick of time! I knew where he was now, and I was at peace. None of us know if there will be a tomorrow!

COLLECTIONS OF THE HEART

Mistaken Impression
by Merry Streeter

Therefore there is now no condemnation for those who are in Christ Jesus.-Romans 8:1

Three years into marriage, I visited an extensive Bible Study within our church. My husband was busy serving, and there was an extra hour in my schedule, so I decided to attend this study. Sitting rather uncomfortably in the metal chair with my very pregnant state easily seen bulging beneath a maternity top, I wished Rick was with me. I was by myself and felt it. After the singing, the teacher asked everyone to gather in groups of two or three to pray for each other. A strange man standing next to me turned and began to pray for my repentance in a prophetic-kind of way. He said out loud to the Lord that I should flee fornication and lust, repent of my sin, and come clean. Appalled and stunned by his words, I stood frozen in disbelief. *What did he say?* The shock was so great I couldn't speak to set the record straight. This shy, naive twenty-one-year-old woman clammed up and promptly left as a dark cloud hovered over me.

The man's words were an unfortunate case of a false prophetic utterance. I *was* married, living a faithful life with my husband expecting our first child. His words made no sense. I could only guess he made an assessment based on his first impression—a young, pregnant woman. I did *look* very young for my already young age, and I was expecting. Never-mind a wedding ring on my finger! I had to deal with the feelings of condemnation, and fortunately, this experience was NOT to be the norm from then on. Soon, knowing I was innocent of those awful words, they fell by the wayside, and I would be prayerful where I found myself next time.

False impressions happen, but we must hide His Word in our hearts should we come into such a situation as I had. We must remember that no matter how someone might make us feel if we are innocent of false words, we can remind ourselves of that fact and not get trapped by false guilt. We can trust His Word and remember that there is now, therefore, NO condemnation for those in Christ Jesus.

MY DREAM VACATION
by Cindy Tesar

"I have come home at last! This is my real country! I belong here. This is the land I have been looking for all my life, though I never knew it till now...Come further up, come further in!"~

The Last Battle (Chronicles of Narnia #7) C.S. Lewis

As she lay dying from a glioblastoma that had eclipsed much of her body function, my mother listened to the testimony of Rebecca Reuter Springer, an excerpt from *My Dream of Heaven*. The old cassette player tended to chew up and spit out offerings that we had to rewind with a Bic pen. We were fortunate to hear the words over and over on a good day. It was a voice much like that of Kathryn Kuhlman, though softer, colored in heavenly tones of awe and wonder. Rebecca recalled her miraculous account of crossing-over to a world enveloped in colorful beauty and endless song. Each entity, each blade of velvety grass, each flower and tree sang its own song in harmony with the ongoing worship to the One Who came to take her hand. Embraced in the glory of His presence, His love, she followed as He led her from the soft, emerald grasses down a pathway of transparent gold across the threshold of what was to be her place, custom prepared. She stepped onto the floor of translucent golden glass blocks in which perfectly formed red roses were suspended. All too soon, she was transported back to the hospital room forty-five minutes after the pronouncement of her death. It was, not yet, her time.

My dream of heaven could not begin to grasp what God has prepared for me (1 Corinthians 2:9). The idea of encountering that 4th dimension of the Spirit, to enter through the very Door, Himself, face-to-face with the Lover of my soul--in the Presence of Truth, Life, Light, Living Water... .is so overwhelming! All earthly senses have primed me for the journey: My eyes (*sight*) will behold Him! I will *taste* the fruit of the Tree of Life, eat heavenly manna, and drink the wine at the Marriage Supper of the Lamb. My voice will join in the heavenly song around the throne with all the glorious company of the saints and angels as we sing, "Holy, holy, holy." My *hearing* was made for that. I will inhale the fragrance of flowers and the wafting scent of incense (*smell*). I will revel in the embrace of loved ones who have gone one before and hold the children I miscarried in this world. I will *touch* and kiss the face of my Savior! It is a dream vacation, to be sure, where no packing is involved, the fare has been

COLLECTIONS OF THE HEART

paid, and air transport is included. Indeed, it is the trip of a lifetime; satisfaction guaranteed! Make room, O my heart, to embrace the wonders of heaven.

The Arm Story
by Reina Dozier

"Wives, submit yourselves to your own husbands as you do to the Lord." -Ephesians 5:22

The word "submit" always seems to leave a bad taste in people's mouths. They associate it with negativity. It's a sore spot for women, and men cringe because they know they will have to hear about it later. As a teen, I remember thinking I will never submit to any man. To "submit" means to be weak. To be submissive means to be lesser than another. At least that is what the world wanted me to think. So could you imagine my hesitation when I asked if I would lead a lesson on this verse, to a room full of ladies? Yikes! But it turned out to be one of the best moments as I submitted to the Lord and said yes.

My right arm is definitely my dominate arm. It seems to do just about everything as compared to my left arm. However, almost a week ago, I did something to my left arm, and it hurts. I always saw my left arm as a recessive or submissive arm. I don't write with my left arm, don't change diapers with my left arm, don't wash dishes with my left arm, etc. However, since it has been hurting, I have realized just how valuable my left arm has been. I have noticed that my left arm is my right arms helper. When my right arm is wiping baby Jr's butt, my left arm is lifting his legs. When my right arm is washing the dish, my left arm is holding the dish. When my right arm is writing, my left arm is holding down the paper. Just like in a marriage, I think the wife is doing all of the holding and lifting. My left arm is just as important as my right arm; it only has a different job then my right one. I can throw farther with my right. I can punch harder with my right. My right arm is physically stronger. But my left arm is the one that hugs my children close to my heart. My left arm is always doing something to assist my right arm. My left arm holds down the fort, so to speak. I thought of this analogy as a husband and wife scenario. My right arm is the husband, and my left arm is the wife. Both arms are valuable to the body. Both arms are useful. Both arms are very different, and that is how God made them. It is supposed to be that way.

    The more I thought about the different roles "head of household" and "assistant," the more I came to realize just how precious the less dominant role really is. I think of the doctor and the nurse. The nurse is the one who cares for the patient. She is just as crucial to the hospital as the doctor. Look at how treasured the women in the Bible were when Jesus spoke of them. Now that we have looked at some different ways to see the word "submit," let us look again at our passage Ephesians 5:22. Thinking of the "arm" story, it doesn't seem so degrading like the world would like us to see it.

The Powerful Flow!
by Merry Streeter

"The words of a [discreet] and wise man's mouth are as deep waters [plenteous and difficult to fathom]; and the fountain of skillful and godly Wisdom is as a gushing stream [sparkling, fresh, pure, and life-giving]." Proverbs 18:4 Amplified Bible

There is something exquisite about a waterfall.

As a group of us hiked Forest Falls one year, we could hear rushing water from a distance. As we drew closer to the source, the mist excited while our eyes dazzled at the sparkling trail. We continued up the rocky dirt path while the incline became treacherous, and we grew tired, but the sound of loud rushing water sent a thrill into our souls to keep us going. Slipping on rocks, we steadied, determined to reach our destination.

After two hours of climb, there she was in all her glory—the surging white falls. We had made it! We had reached her! Some wanted to go right under it, some wanted to touch the misty edge, some just wanted to look at it from a distance, but we all enjoyed the bliss of the powerful pounding flow!

And just like that, the sound & power of wisdom has its rush. Sometimes like cold pulsating falls rushing over our heads when we are dry, empty, and tired, sensible words refresh and give us "Ahhhhhhh!"

The powerful flow of wise words lifts us when we are distressed. They give direction and purpose when we feel aimless. It straightens a crooked path when we're weaving in and out; hope when we have none. Are there any better words than those?

Gaining wisdom or finding others who speak it are also likened to finding a waterfall. Not easy to get to, yet with effort and a seeking heart, it is reachable.

COLLECTIONS OF THE HEART

Lord, you said in the book of James, "But if any of you lacks wisdom, let him ask of God, who gives to all generously and without reproach, and it will be given to him." So we ask you now in our current situation, to give wisdom. We need to know what to do, when to do it, and how. You have all those answers wrapped in heavenly wisdom. We ask it now, looking up with confidence, in Jesus' name.

HUMOR

SPIN-THE-BOTTLE
by Jim Hutcheson

On a hot fall day in 1944, I was sitting in the fifth-grade classroom very bored. A fellow student, Phillis, was reading to the class from our geography book about life along the Nile River in ancient times with reed boats, bulrushes, and crocodiles. Amy, a cute blond girl with long pigtails, sat in front of me. She was tired and kept stretching and slouching in her seat. Her pigtail happened to dropped down next to my inkwell. I merely pushed it in.

Startled, she swung her head around, and ink flew everywhere. She blurted, very angrily, "Jimmie, I hate you. I'll never speak to you again."

By now, Mrs. Lee, our teacher, was at our desks. She told Sue, another classmate, to go with Amy to the restroom and help her wash the ink out of her hair and blouse. Mrs. Lee commanded, "Keep the pigtail away from your blouse, or the ink will stain it."

Turning and looking at me, she said, "Why did you do that?"

"Her pigtail just happened to fall into my inkwell." She raised one eyebrow. Mrs. Lee did not believe me. The recess bell rang, and she dismissed the class except for me.

"Go get some wet and dry paper towels and clean up this mess before it dries; and wash the ink out of your shirt!"

"Yes, Ma'am." The ink on my desk cleaned up well, my geography book was stained but still usable, and the ink might wash out of my shirt.

Mrs. Lee looked at me sternly and said, "Get your pen and some paper and write this sentence 100 times. Your penmanship better be good with no miss spelled words, or you will stay after class and rewrite. I will correct your papers after class today. The sentence is: I will not antagonize the girls in this class again. Do you understand me?"

"Yes, Ma'am."

I had to stay for about 45 min. after school to finish my punishment, and then I hurried home. Mom thought that I was late playing with some of the guys. Fortunately, I did not have to take a note home and have it signed, or I would have been grounded for a month.

About two weeks later, Phillis handed me an invitation to her birthday party. I asked, "Who are all coming?"

COLLECTIONS OF THE HEART

She answered, "Barbra, Alice, Amy, Rose and me, for the girls and boys, Pat, Charlie, Jack, Ernie, and you."

Is this pairing up? Aw, with these guys, it will be ok. The party was scheduled for the next Friday evening from 6-9 PM—cake, ice-cream, games, etc. *What kind of games can 10 kids play together?*

Friday, when I came home from school, mom made me go in and take a bath and put on all clean clothes so I would look respectable.

The guys aren't going to do this, so why am I? Oh well, if it makes mom happy, ok. Mom fixed me an early supper so that I wouldn't be late for the party. I didn't quite make it by 6 PM, but I was there by 6:15.

Mom's parting words were, " Don't forget the present and tell Mrs. Carter hello for me and that we need to have coffee together soon and when you leave to come home, tell Mr. and Mrs. Carter as well as Phillis, thank you for a nice party and you had a good time."

Once arrived, I looked around, and there were only girls in their frilly dresses! But where were all the guys? I soon found out that there was a football game that night between the Decader Gladiators and Mohomet Bulldogs, and they all

COLLECTIONS OF THE HEART

deserted me for the game. *Five girls and one boy. Now what?* The girls decided to go to the backyard for some games.

They decided to play "Spin-The-Bottle." I do not know if we played by the right rules or not. You sit down in a circle, and since I was the only boy, naturally I was Post Master. Phillis got a bottle and a board to spin it on. To start the game, I made the first spin. The person it points to then mails a letter and spins the bottle to find the next person to mail a letter.

SAGA OF TWO HORNS
By Jim Hutcheson

In the late 1930s-40s, a common belief was that playing a musical instrument would help a young person develop socially and be more disciplined. In 1945, while living in Champaign, Illinois, the city had a band program for young musicians during summer vacation. We were all encouraged to bring an instrument and join in.

Having had a bad experience four years before learning to play the guitar, I was now going to play the trumpet. The band room was wide with a three-tier riser. From the front, stringed instruments were on the left and woodwinds and percussions on the right. My trumpet position was middle-tier four seats right of center. Right behind me was a trombone player.

After several sessions and a little warm-up, the conductor tapped his baton, had us take our seats, and we began to make noise. To me, it was noise because it did not sound much like music. Twice, during these early sessions, the trombonist' slide hit me, once in the back of my head and then in my back. This really didn't hurt, but it did irritate me.

At a later session, the trombonist, while playing, hit my shoulder and his spit valve on the lower end of the slide came open, making his notes go very sour. The conductor came to us and gave him the riot act wanting to know what is going on? I learned that the spring on the spit valve was broken and would stay open at a slight touch.

Several sessions later, I had the opportunity to covertly open that spit valve, and his notes went very sour. The conductor spoke to him again, very tersely. Some of the girls were giggling, and the guys cutting up, and he was mad. I knew I would get that slide in my back someplace, but I remembered my cousin as I opened the valve.

My uncle Charlie had made a nice display around the Christmas tree, HO train, tunnels, bridges, town, etc. Bobby, my cousin, was watching the train go around. Uncle Charlie told him, "If you touch it, you will get a spanking." On the third or fourth round, we could hear Bobby mumbling to himself, "If I doed it I get a whipping,...If I doed it I get a whipping....If I doed it I get a whipping." Just then, the engine came out of the tunnel. Bobby, "I doed it!!" grabbed the engine knocking the cars off the track. Uncle Charlie gave him one swat just hard enough to hurt his dignity but maybe he will remember it.

I knew I was going to get that slide in my back, but...."I doed it." Only you can weigh whether the punishment is greater than the enjoyment. In this case, enjoyment won.

Where Is Nowhere
by Jim Hutcheson

As we were getting ready to start our journey to find **Nowhere,** Mr. Rogers came by and asked, "Where are you going?" I replied, "To a place called **Nowhere**. Can you direct me to it? "

He thought for a moment and said, "Now let me see. If you go straight east, no, that won't get you there. West; that won't work either, straight north; south; no. A diagonal; won't work either. Your best bet is this meandering road."

COLLECTIONS OF THE HEART

We started our journey one step at a time, and after several miles, we met a little red-headed girl in a red dress carrying a basket. I asked, "Are we on the right road to *Nowhere*?" She replied, "How do I know. I only know the way to grandma's house." I thanked her, and we continued, and since the sun was getting ready to set, we camped in the edge of the woods by a babbling brook.

The next morning just after sunrise, we continued our journey, and near noon we came across Mr. Tinman. I asked, "How are your joints?" He said, "Now that they have been oiled, they are fine. I can swing my ax freely."

I ask, "Are we on the right road to *Nowhere*?" … "No," he replied, "Follow this yellow brick road back to the fork and take the one marked "Ends of the Earth." When you get there, it is just a hop, a skip, and a jump to *Nowhere*." I thanked him, and we moved on.

After several more miles, the trees began to thin and we could see meadows, rolling hills, and mountains way off in the distance. It was now getting late, so we camped in the meadow by a beautiful trout stream.

Rising early, we continued our quest and after several miles, we saw a police patrol car behind some bushes watching the road. As we passed the officer hailed us, "Where you all going?" I replied, "To the "Ends of the Earth" and from there to *Nowhere*."

He pulled up next to us and said, "That's a pretty fair piece from here. Since things are slow, hop in and I'll give you all a lift." After thirty-some miles, we arrived at our first destination, "Ends of the Earth."

As we got out of the patrol car the officer said, "Tell Mr. Zoe, that I brung ya and that he better hep ya'll get to *Nowhere*." We thanked the officer and went in to see Mr. Zoe.

"Mr. Zoe, the officer told us to tell you that he brought us and that you would help us get to *Nowhere*. We were told that *Nowhere* is just a hop, skip, and a jump from here. How do we get there?"

"Weeelll now, let me see, *Nowhere* is out of my jurisdiction. I'm gonna have to send you to "Intergalactic Informational Services and talk to Colonel Weatherbee. See that white telephone out there by the gate. Go dial 7734 and he'll answer."

"This is Intergalactic Informational Services, Colonel Weathebee speaking. How may I help you?"

I replied, "Can you help us get to *Nowhere*?"

COLLECTIONS OF THE HEART

"*Nowhere*…. *Nowhere*, let me see, I think I have heard of it. I'll put it into the computer and see where it is located." We heard a lot of beep…beep…beep…bong…bong and then dit, dit, dit, dit.

"I've found it. *Nowhere* is the third planet of NCI-527 in the constellation of Leo and only 5.2 light-years away. We don't have much time, so I am going to send my driver to the gate to pick you up. He will bring you here and then take you to launchpad seventeen which has a rocket which will be launched in three days."

The driver took us to Colonel Weatherbee to sign some forms and then to launchpad seventeen to Flight Commander Harrington.

Commander Harrington began briefing us on the flight and what to expect. Looking at space displays on his computer he said, "We cannot fly a direct course to a point in space to intercept *Nowhere* because we would fly too close to a black hole. However, by flying to NCI-304-2, its second planet, will then slingshot us on a direct flight to *Nowhere* and increase our speed by a factor of three. This will reduce our flight time considerably."

The Commander called Chief Master Sargent Ablemon told him to issue us space suits and all the necessary equipment

COLLECTIONS OF THE HEART

that we will need for this flight and to brief us on the crew capsule and lander.

Sargent Ablemon took us to the crew capsule and explained that during launch we would hear a roar and feel some vibration. "Don't worry, he said, this is normal. You will be in a sitting position with your backs towards the earth looking straight up and strapped in. One hour before you reach the speed of light a drawer will open. It will have three capsules and three plastic bags of water. Swallow the capsules and water immediately. Change your chairs to horizontal beds, lay down, and engage the belt strap. Within ninety seconds of swallowing the capsule, you will be asleep in suspended animation. You will stay in this position until you are near *Nowhere*. Then we'll wake you. If you fail to take the capsule to go into suspended animation your body will age quickly, and you will expire. So, be sure you take it on time."

"Upon waking, transfer to the lander, put on your helmet, open the oxygen valve, and close the lander's hatch. At the correct time, we will deploy the lander and its retro rockets will slow your descent down to a soft landing."

When the lander has landed turn the toggle switch labeled "Communications" to the "On" position and leave it on. This allows ground control to talk to you and you to talk to each other and ground control even when you are away from the lander.

When you turn the switch on you will receive these final instructions. One, synchronize your watches to the same time, to the minute, to the clock in the lander. Two, the lander will be on *Nowhere* for only <u>seventy-two hours and eleven minutes</u>. At that time, it will launch and fly up to the mothership. You <u>must</u> be onboard one hour before liftoff or you **will** be left behind. **Is that understood? There are no exceptions.**

The landers hatch will not open until you push the red button above the hatch indicating all systems "go" for your new atmosphere. Now you can open the hatch and put your foot on a new planet."

When we opened the hatch and looked around, *Nowhere* seems to be a dead planet. There was no vegetation growing nor any sign of dead growth. There were no tracks of any life in the dust on the surface. Walking over to some rocks there seem to be the remains of a very ancient streambed, now dry. In the dust, there were indications of where meteorites had hit the surface and a short way away from a crater from a meteor.

COLLECTIONS OF THE HEART

Nightfall presented a real challenge because the rocks and dust glowed just like uranium in the presence of ultraviolet light. The colors were beautiful but very eerie. The next day was spent taking many pictures and gathering rock samples. We found a small empty drawer in the lander to hold our rocks.

Day three our search was short because we wanted to make sure we were on board the lander with the hatch closed ready for liftoff well before time to depart. At minus two hours, ground control contacted us to make sure we were ready.

At seventy-two hours eleven minutes and seven seconds, the lander blasted off from *Nowhere* and was captured by the mother ship. We transferred to the crew capsule, took our suspended animation capsules, and went to bed. We woke up just before entering the earth's atmosphere and making a vertical landing at the "Intergalactic Informational Services complex."

Life now seems very weird. We have only aged about a week, but it is now one hundred, fourteen years, seven months, and five days since we left for *Nowhere*. All our friends are gone, and nothing is the same.

Nowhere has to be somewhere and there can be a place called Nowhere, but where?

COLLECTIONS OF THE HEART

PROPHETIC

Eschatology
by Jim Hutcheson

The farther I travel down the highway of life, the more I appreciate the study of eschatology. Eschatology is a highbrow word with a straightforward meaning.

> The dictionary meaning of eschatology: The branch of theology that is concerned with the ultimate or last things, such as death, judgment, heaven, and hell.

As a Christian, this can be simplified: things to come and prophesies fulfilled or not yet fulfilled.

There are many prophecies; however, I am only addressing two that are relevant to today.

> The 1st. a covenant that was given to Abraham by God. Gen 12: 3, **"I will bless those who bless you and whoever curses you I will curse, and all the people on earth will be blessed through you."** This covenant has never been revoked. It was given c 2000 BC.

Three of our recent administrations have tried to throw Israel under the bus. It would be better for The United States if we observed this covenant than to suffer the consequences.

When we read in the Old Testament and see how God dealt with Israel when they turned their back on Him, are we, or will we, receive the same judgment for doing the same things?

> The 2nd. In both the Old and New Testaments, there are references to signs in the sky to get our attention. Joel 2:31 ***"The sun will turn to darkness and the moon to blood before the coming and dreadful day of the Lord."*** Acts 2:20 ***"The sun will turn to darkness and the moon to blood before the coming of the great and glorious day of the Lord"*** and Rev. 6:12 ***"I watched as he opened the sixth seal. There was a great earthquake. The sun turned black like sackcloth made of goat hair; the whole moon turned blood red..."*** Recently there have been many disasters such as earthquakes, floods, fires, droughts, volcano eruptions, etc. Could these be related to this prophecy?

The significant blood moons are called blood moons or a tetrad (a series of four consecutive lunar eclipses, coinciding on Jewish Holidays, with six full moons between, and no intervening partial lunar eclipses). We are presently waiting for the last or 4th moon of this present series. The last blood moon of this series will be on 28 Sept. 2015.

COLLECTIONS OF THE HEART

A tetrad or blood moon series' appeared just before the Pope sent a letter to King Ferdinand of Spain, telling him to expel all the Jews, to give them one week to go or be executed. All property left by the Jews was to become the property of the church in Rome.

Several wealthy Jews commissioned and outfitted Christopher Columbus, a Jew, to seek a place where they could worship in peace. Thus in 1492, new land was discovered.

The next tetrad was in 1948 when Israel became a new nation, and Jews worldwide began to return to their homeland. Zech. 10: *9 "Though I scatter them among the peoples, yet in distant lands, they will remember me. They and their children will survive, and they will return."*

The next tetrad was in 1967, "The 6 Day War" between Israel and Egypt, Jordan, and Syria.

There has been a lot of speculation about the present four blood moons as to where or what God will do. Speculation runs the gamut from the beginning of the seven years of tribulation to WWIII, a new local war in the middle east, and/or the king of the north attacking

Israel because Israel is now energy self-sufficient and no longer needs coal, oil, or LNG from Russia.

Deut. 33: 19 *"They will summon peoples to the mountain and there offer sacrifices of righteousness; they will feast on the abundance of the seas, on the treasures hidden in the sand."* Three vast very rich oil/gas deposits off the coast of Haifa and five on the shore south of Haifa will supply Israel with enough natural gas to power its electrical plants and provide commercial and domestic to other countries for the foreseeable future. This will/has cut very sharply into Putin's bottom line. What will he do?

Have the oil/gas discoveries fulfilled this prophecy in Deut.33:19?

AUTHORS
(IN ALPHABETICAL ORDER)

Phyllis Boles

Believing God's beauty displays all aspects of our lives encourages Phyllis to write. She desires to encourage readers to see the beauty of His manuscript by creatively crafting thoughts on paper.

She is a lover of reading, writing, and journaling.

Phyllis began writing poetry in elementary school. Like many girls, she began writing in her diary as a teenager, which has now evolved into journaling. In her twenties, she entered a songwriting contest and was excited to make it to the second round. A few years ago, she collaborated with other moms to develop a purity curriculum for young ladies at her church. She has also written encouraging lessons with other authors for the book "Rescue: A Homeschool Mom's Devotion."

She is a former high school teacher for government, economics, and speech and debate. She currently works as an Administrative Assistant and Mentor for Forgotten Children Inc. at Rachel's House of Healing—a residential home for women who have been trafficked into prostitution.

Phyllis is usually reading two to three books at the same time with more books on her nightstand waiting to be opened. Her motto is, "Widen your horizons, read books."

You can find her writings at www.tapestryofbeauty.com

COLLECTIONS OF THE HEART

Reina Dozier

Reina Dozier is a first-time author but long-time writer. She loves Jesus, is married to her high school sweetheart, and is blessed to stay at home with their children, pouring into their lives each day. Reina is a trucker's wife, a homeschool mom, and a grandma to five grandbabies in Heaven. She also cares for a TV-watching pet bearded dragon.

Reina is a little bubble of stories. In 2012 the Lord put upon her heart the title of a book and said, "Write." The book title "We Put the Fun in Dysfunctional" grew into a book series that she continues to work on. She published her first book, "Ground Zero," August 18, 2020, which you can find on Amazon.com.

Jim Hutcheson

Jim served in the USAF from 1952-56, two years as a base photographer, and two years as a crew chief on a B47 bomber. Wanting a better photographic knowledge, he earned his BA in professional arts from Brooks Institute of Photography in Santa Barbara, Ca., graduating in the spring class of 1959. To better his electronic background, he studied electronics at Chaffey Jr, College, Cucamonga, Ca. at night.

He worked for General Dynamics in Pomona and Cucamonga for over 33 years. He was a motion picture/ video/a.v./photo instrumentation specialist. He has worked in every aspect of motion picture and video productions. He was a writer/rewriter of scripts, director, cameraman, soundman, and editor. He was the lead man in charge of video productions having everything in a small to medium-size television station except for the end transmitter. Classified material does not get transmitted under normal conditions.

He worked on systems for use in outer space, air-to-air, air-to-ground, ground-to-air missiles, gun systems, underwater systems, and systems that don't exist.

While working, he had two articles published in a national magazine, "Photo Methods for Industry." The first is estimating the cost of a motion picture/video production, so you don't go broke. The second is an interface circuit to allow you to go from a high-level output to a low-level input without overdriving the system.

Now since he is retired, he writes reports, scripts, and short stories as God directs him. His prayer has been and will always be, "Lord, put your words in my mouth, no mine, put your thoughts in my mind so I can put them on paper and use me for Your glory, not mine. Thank you, Lord Jesus."

Dennis Knotts

Dennis Knotts joined the Church when he was eight years old. He was even baptized but did not personally ask Jesus to save him until he graduated high school. In 1977, Dennis died in an auto accident, but as he watched the paramedics work on his body, Jesus told him, "You're not done yet." Dennis was sent back. God was merciful to him, and He gave Dennis the gift of writing. He called him to a puppet ministry and a drama ministry. He gave Dennis a wonderful wife, Beverly. They both worked in Children Ministries over the years and continued performing with puppets. God gave him two beautiful daughters: Tanya, whom God brought home to live with Him on the day of her birth, and Shalom, who has a love for books and writing. He is currently retired and continues to write as a ministry. You can find his books on Amazon.com

amazon.com/author/dennis-knotts

COLLECTIONS OF THE HEART

Stella McDowell

Stella didn't intend to become an author. She wrote the story of her parents to introduce them and the Gospel to the following generations. Early readers of her story said it needed to go further than just the family, so she self-published her book, "Leaving Tracks in the Snow." Feedback came with examples of how the book touched people's lives and with repeated statements, "you're a good writer." Her attitude is, if God gives you a gift, you are responsible for using it. She continues to write and has been published in LIVE.

She went to SoCal Christian Writer's conference in 2018. The memoir presenter there, Robin Grunder, looked through her book and told her she needed to be teaching others how to write their family and faith stories. She went home, told her pastor, and he agreed. "Let's schedule you for a two-hour workshop two and a half months from now." Since then, she has been presenting workshops and has become an advocate for others to preserve their stories.

Her parents claimed at a late age, "We're not retired, just retreaded." Stella may be a retired nurse and grandma, but she's retreaded, and on this new journey of preserving stories.

Her verse for this season of her life is Psalms 71:18.

stellamcdowellauthor@gmail.com

COLLECTIONS OF THE HEART

Sharon Miller

Sharon Miller is a retired Elementary School teacher who lives with her cat, Princess, in Moreno Valley. She accepted Christ as her savior at the age of six- and one-half years old but finds herself daily in need of a closer walk with him. As a result, God has laid on her heart to write for her nieces, ages four to eight, tweens in search of encouragement, and whatever else He leads her to pen. Other works are poems, short stories, and is currently drafting a book (see excerpt) specially written to edify foster teens ages ten to fourteen. Her wish is to leave a legacy of encouragement.

Merry S. Streeter

Born in Denmark, Merry arrived in Southern California in 1961. During the early '70s-Jesus-Movement surrendered her life to the Lord Jesus Christ. She began sharing her faith after the baptism of the Holy Spirit. At nineteen, she was called by God to teach Bible stories to children and lead them to worship Him.

Greatly encouraged by her family, the women at her church, and other authors, Merry has published two children's books with a few more on the burner. Her first picture book called *Lolly's Fish Tale; When She Meets A Bully Face to Face,* she illustrated. Her talented daughter, Kelly Galusha, brought Merry's drawings to life with digital color and texture. Her second book, *Apollumi, Journey to The Great King,* is a short story to lead children in pursuit of their Great King. She has two more children's books in progress, often thinking of her grandchildren while she writes.

Merry continues to share her faith in writing because she says, "Jesus is everything! Someone told me about Him; I must tell others." To see her books go to:
amazon.com/author/merrystreeter

COLLECTIONS OF THE HEART

Cindy Tesar

Inspirational author, CINDY TESAR, embraces journaling to catch the sweet drips of fellowship with the Lord. She's encouraged the Body of Christ for over 35 years. She writes chiefly so that others might know their God-given gifts, identity, and purpose. She develops Bible curriculum, devotionals, and fiction for children of all ages, including adults. She and husband Mike, reside in Hemet, CA. They have been married 51 years, have four married adult children, thirteen grandkids, and two-great grandkids.

COLLECTIONS OF THE HEART

Made in the USA
Middletown, DE
23 December 2020